Beyond Leadership to Followership

Learning to lead from where you are

Sviatoslav Steve Seteroff, DBA

© Copyright 2003 Sviatoslav Steve Seteroff, DBA. All rights reserved.

No part of this publication may be reproduced, stored in a retrieval system, or transmitted, in any form or by any means, electronic, mechanical, photocopying, recording, or otherwise, without the written prior permission of the author.

Brief extracts may be made for purpose of inclusion in reviews if accompanied by a complete citation and a copy of the review is transmitted to the author or publisher.

Portions have been used as lecture notes © 1997 - 2003.

```
National Library of Canada Cataloguing in Publication

Seteroff, Sviatoslav Steve, 1937-
     Beyond leadership to followership / Sviatoslav Steve Seteroff.
ISBN 1-4120-0816-6
     I. Title.
HM1261.S47 2003         303.3'4              C2003-903927-7
```

This book was published *on-demand* in cooperation with Trafford Publishing.
On-demand publishing is a unique process and service of making a book available for retail sale to the public taking advantage of on-demand manufacturing and Internet marketing. **On-demand publishing** includes promotions, retail sales, manufacturing, order fulfilment, accounting and collecting royalties on behalf of the author.

Suite 6E, 2333 Government St., Victoria, B.C. V8T 4P4, CANADA
  Phone   250-383-6864   Toll-free   1-888-232-4444 (Canada & US)
  Fax   250-383-6804   E-mail   sales@trafford.com
  Web site   www.trafford.com   TRAFFORD PUBLISHING IS A DIVISION OF TRAFFORD HOLDINGS LTD.
  Trafford Catalogue #03-1184   www.trafford.com/robots/03-1184.html

10   9   8   7   6   5   4   3   2   1

Beyond Leadership to Followership: Learning to lead from where you are

Sviatoslav Steve Seteroff, DBA

Table of Contents

Table of Contents iii
Table of Figures vi
Table of Tables vi
Acknowledgements vii
Introduction: The Compass 1
Getting Started: The Map 3
   Where to Begin: A Dilemma 3
   Management – Leadership Continuum 5
   Organizational Learning 6
   Systems Thinking 7
   Teams and Workgroups 8
   Followership 9
   Mentorship 10
   Stewardship and Servant Leadership 11
   Protégée 12
   Supervise 13
   Manage 14
   Tying it all together 14
Management – Leadership Continuum 15
   Historical Aspect of Management 16
   Current Application of Management Theory 18
   Planning for Leadership 20
   The Bottom Line 22
Organizational Learning 23
   Organizational Structure 23
      Organization of the Clan 24
      Fiefdom 25
      Hierarchical Structure 27
      Market Driven Organization Structures 29
   Additional Thoughts on Organizations 33
      Leadership Practice 34
      Dance of Blind Reflex 35

- Implications for Managers 36
- Systems Thinking 39
  - Personal Mastery 41
  - Mental Models 43
  - Shared Vision 44
  - Team Learning 45
  - Systems Thinking 46
  - Implementing a Systems Approach 47
  - Barry Oshry's View 48
    - Environmental Impact 51
    - Approaches to Ensure Survival 52
    - Overlooked Processes of Survival 53
    - Breakdown of Relationships 53
    - Additional Thoughts 53
- Teams 55
  - What are teams? 55
  - Most teams begin as work groups 57
  - High performance work groups 58
  - The beginning of a team structure 59
  - Defining a high performance team 59
  - Organizational Support 60
  - The Implications of Teams 61
- From Leadership to Followership, At Last 62
- Mentorship 65
  - Advisory Role 66
  - Providing Access 66
  - Training and Education 67
  - Encouragement 68
- Stewardship and Servant Leadership 69
  - Servant Leadership is not new. 69
  - Stewardship 71
- Protégée 73
  - Trust 73
  - Loyalty 74
    - Personal Loyalty 74
    - Organizational Loyalty 75
  - Selecting a Mentor 76
- Supervise 77
  - Established and Respected Authority 77
    - Technical Competence 78
    - Well Respected 78
    - Administrative Capabilities 79
  - Administrative Supervisor 80
  - Training Opportunity 81

> Relationship to Workers 81
>
> Manage 83
>> Policy 84
>>> Information gathering 85
>>> SWOT Analysis 85
>>> Dynamic SWOT 87
>>> Formulation 89
>>> Implementation 89
>>> Evaluation and control 90
>> Management in Action 91
>
> Learning Throughout The Process 92
> References 95
> About the Author 97

Table of Figures

Figure 1. Learning and Sharing Knowledge 4
Figure 2. The Management - Leadership Continuum 15
Figure 3. The Leadership - Management Relationship 18
Figure 4. Creating Future Leaders Takes Time and Effort 21
Figure 5. Clan Structure 25
Figure 6. Fiefdom has a single strong leader 26
Figure 7. A Typical Hierarchical Structure 28
Figure 8. Classic Supply and Demand Schedule 29
Figure 9. Many forces act on us 49
Figure 10. A Progression of Work Groups to High Performance Teams 56
Figure 11. Team Building Process (Used with permission of Carl Adams) 57
Figure 12. Traditional SWOT Analysis Matrix 86
Figure 13. Dynamic SWOT Model 87

Table of Tables

Table 1. Matrix of Peter Senge's Five Disciplines 40
Table 2. Oshry's Table of Values 51

Acknowledgements

In the first place, there is absolutely no telling where I would be today without the active and cooperative support of my wife of many years, Joyce. Without her active participation in my success I would probably still be engaged in the more unproductive activities of my youth. I owe my thirst for knowledge to many people along the way who have encouraged me and supported my often bizarre behavior while attempting to learn as much as possible. I have learned so much from so many and each has formed an inseparable part of my being. If any single group is deserving of contributing more than another, it would have to be my adult graduate students who learn so quickly that there really is no single undisputed authority on any subject and that we should challenge everything we see, hear, taste, smell, or feel. From each I continue to learn. Thank you.

Introduction: The Compass

The traditional approach to leadership is that it must be from the top down to be effective, and perhaps that is the ideal approach. However, what are we, at lower levels of our organizations, to do when we see the need for leadership and change in our own organization but do not have the support of our hierarchical superiors to make the change a reality? Perhaps all is not lost, and there is an approach we can use to effectively undertake the change process.

We each function within parameters set by our organization. At the highest level, whether for-profit, non-profit, or public agency, we are responsible for the performance of our organization to our boards of directors, agency heads, or in the highest case the electorate that placed us in the role we are in. At the lowest levels we are subject to work rules, process instructions, and specific direction. In each case we are free to operate within the parameters established for our position and task to be performed. The benefit is that our parameters are either clearly defined, well established, or can be inferred with some accuracy and reliability. It is these parameters that allow us to create for ourselves a leadership role wherever we find ourselves in the organization.

To understand our options, we must briefly visit the approaches to leadership because we will use the same knowledge available to those at the top of our organizations to enhance our own value at whatever level we may be. More importantly, we hope that through judicious application of these principles, we will not only perform better but will also make our performance so recognizable as to allow us to move up the promotion ladder. It is not an easy task and if someone tells you it is, run like the wind before you are trapped into self delusion. Remember that if it sounds too good to be true, you can count on it to be so.

So what does this slender volume offer you?

We present a brief overview of the theory and a few tools behind implementation of management and leadership principles. Hopefully, we add some clarity on the meaning of teams. We also take a few side trips to ensure that we understand that what we are undertaking is achievable, regardless of where we find ourselves in an organization.

We will not attempt to present a prescription.

There is no single right way to implement leadership practice, and there is no single road map to success. There is knowledge. There is intelligence. This book assists in pointing to the knowledge. You must provide the intelligence.

Getting Started: The Map

Recently, a mature graduate student in a leadership workshop raised a question that has inspired me to further research and managed to excite me more than I could have believed possible. This graduate student, Nicholas Boechler, pointed out that if the definition of a leader was one that had followers, what was the description of a follower? He went on to observe that there seem to be plenty of academic articles, books, and popular press articles on leadership, but he had not managed to find a single recent article on followership. After some reflection, we all agreed that we too had not seen a definition of followership or any articles on how to be a better follower. Needless to say, this began a quest for more knowledge on the subject and managed to occupy our time for several weeks as we kept returning to this topic in an attempt to gain clarity about leadership. Much of our dialogue on this issue and the research is included in this work because it has become apparent to me that we cannot address leadership without examining followership.

Where to Begin: A Dilemma

The problem facing scholars as well as practitioners of leadership and management is the approach to take when there does not appear to be a logical progression, or even a related series of disciplines that can be considered separately. This very trans-disciplinary, or systems (Bertalanffy, 1969), approach popularized by Peter Senge (Senge, 1990; Senge, 1994; Senge et al., 1999) makes it difficult to find a place to begin. The position taken here is one that is perhaps pragmatic, rather than systematic, by following our title and starting where we are the most familiar and bringing in areas of concern as they emerge to relevance. Since this is not a prescriptive approach and we encourage the reader to browse at will. This should not pose a major structural problem for either of us.

If we accept the premise of James Nolan (Nolan, 1984) that leadership and followership are of equal importance, we must look to earlier work that suggested a progression of leadership - teamship - followership as an appropriate continuum. Perhaps at this early point in our journey we should look briefly at one approach that has caused me to take a closer look at the leadership process.

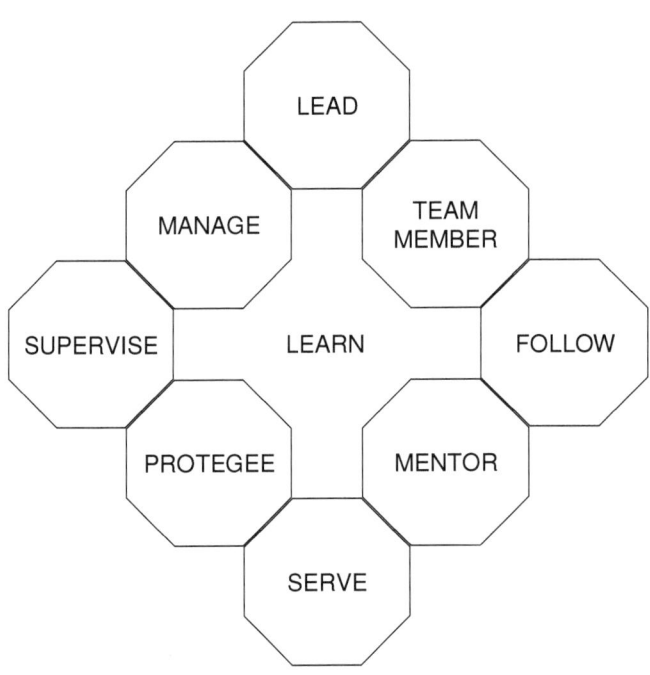

Figure 1. Learning and Sharing Knowledge

You have picked up this volume for a reason. Hopefully it is the thirst for knowledge that bites each one of us sooner or later in life. We call this learning. Learning however, is sterile unless shared. This sharing has become the cornerstone of our effort to maintain organizational integrity. When applied, we can retain the hard won competitive edge of our knowledge workers by creating a learning organization (Argyris, 1975). As you continue through this volume, learning will remain central to our discourse.

Management – Leadership Continuum

Confusion between management and leadership has created havoc in some organizations because they are not applied consistently or uniformly. We expect leaders in our organizations to possess magical attributes based on their positional title and be able to answer any question. Managers are seen as lesser leaders and are limited to total knowledge only in their own areas of responsibility, with perhaps some retention of knowledge from other areas where they had served. In reality, we are all faced with doubts, aspirations, and search for the knowledge to do the right thing, regardless of where we find ourselves in the organization at the moment. For this very reason, we can emerge as leaders wherever we may find ourselves, providing we understand the fundamental principles and learn from those who have pioneered. Understanding that we must be managers and leaders simultaneously is a beginning. Understanding the principles involved in both management and leadership can assist us in determining the proper mix at a point in time that is appropriate for our position within the organization. When examining the theories, it would be well to remember that in any position, we are bound by formally and informally established parameters yet may have great flexibility to exercise leadership and management approaches within the existing scope of our responsibilities.

Organizational Learning

In the past, individuals considered knowledge to be power and the tendency was to hoard the hard earned knowledge, both as a means of ensuring job security and to enhance personal standing within the organization. Sharing of knowledge was carefully controlled. Indeed, this approach is still practiced in many organizations and becomes the chief stumbling block to achieving a highly competitive position in an increasingly fast-paced operating environment. Companies today compete for market share and profits by aggressively reducing the cost of doing business, and non-profit organizations compete for declining sources of revenue by delivering more services at a lower cost.

In the past, we joined a company or non-profit organization and remained with it for our working life, rising as openings became available on the basis of seniority or connections. As our organizations became bloated and the global competitive environment advanced at an accelerated pace, we found that we could no longer support the heavy burden of overhead costs and remain competitive. Several factors began to play a vital role in the effort to reduce costs; pressure from investors for greater profits, pressure from the workforce for increased compensation, pressure from consumers for lower costs, and consumer sophistication in obtaining product comparative data among them. If we subscribe to the economics based approach that profit is equal to total revenue minus total cost, we begin to realize that the informed consumer will quickly determine the market price of the product or service we are offering, so to increase profits, we must reduce cost. In each case, the driver is to reduce cost and we have found that the cost of people constitutes a large part of the cost of doing business, even in volunteer-based, non-profit, organizations. As our effective workforce continues to shrink, the need to create and maintain a learning organization where the individual is rewarded for superior performance, as well as for increasing the performance of all within the organization begins to take on a survival perspective for both the individual and the organization. The individual benefit derives from the acquisition of knowledge and an increase in marketability when, not if, another position is sought. The organization benefits from an open exchange of knowledge because when the individual inevitably leaves the organization, the knowledge possessed by the individual remains within the organization in an applied sense. The trick is to continue to survive using existing management practices while positioning for the future by applying leadership principles and learning to apply systems thinking.

Systems Thinking

We have long known that the greater our understanding of the total environment the better the quality of our decisions. However, it was not until the late 1960's that a comprehensive academic approach was taken to better our understanding of the possibilities that open when we take a holistic approach, and encourage those about us to do the same.

It makes very little difference whether we are engaged in a for profit venture in manufacturing or service industry, an independent consultancy, as a public servant, or laboring in a non-profit organization. The better we understand the operational environment and the factors that bear on it, the better the quality of our decisions. The issue then becomes how to accumulate this vast amount of knowledge necessary to achieve such an ambitious outcome. Clearly no single individual can accomplish this in a reasonable period of time;

however, if we can form an organizational structure that supports organizational learning and an ability to share our hard won knowledge, it becomes much easier. When a majority of members in an organization can take a holistic approach we begin to shift from a multi-disciplinary to a trans-disciplinary approach to problem solving, resulting in the higher quality decision process that supports rapid and appropriate response to emergent operational issues.

What began, in the modern era, with Bertalanffy (Bertalanffy, 1969) as a theoretical concept, was moved into a more practical direction by Peter Checkland (Checkland, 1993) and more importantly in chaos theory by Margaret Wheatley (Wheatley & Kellner-Rogers, 1996) who suggested that when we take a simpler approach to problem solving we reduce the potential for error that is inherent in complex approaches to problem solving. The better known approach, and one that has been embraced by many business and non-profit organization leaders, and most universities, is the Fifth Discipline and the subsequent works of Peter Senge (Senge, 1990; Senge, 1991; Senge, 1994; Senge, 1996; Senge et al., 1999).

One would think that with all this academic and practitioner effort, we would be well on the way toward understanding the concepts involved, yet we are reminded time and again that we have forgotten to note that systems thinking is a process and not an event. When we think we have implemented systems thinking, we realize that we have only just begun.

Teams and Workgroups

Current business thought leans heavily toward the implementation of teams for almost any reason whatsoever, and across several organizational structures, but we often fail to understand the power that we are unleashing, or respect the commitment of resources that such an implementation entails. Most heads of organizations are enamored with the idea of teams because of the results they are capable of delivering, but frequently feel threatened as the desired teams begin to evolve from a work group to a team, yet this process is probably one of the easiest to identify potential leaders for additional attention and promotion. Implementing teams is also a good way to justify the additional training and education as it can be clearly tied to a direct need and hopefully an appropriate result for the investment. In an organization that has implemented the team concept, it becomes easier for individuals assigned to work groups, or teams, to begin to emerge as leaders and gain greater visibility in the process. This emergence is not without cost.

What we usually see formed are cross-disciplinary work groups, under the generic title of team, but we must look carefully at the structure, responsibilities, roles, and actions of the members to determine where the group stands on their way to becoming a team. However, if the organization as a whole has adopted a learning organization approach and has embraced systems thinking at a fairly broad level, the transition from workgroup to team is facilitated and each member can emerge as a situational leader when needed.

Followership

As leaders emerge in teams, or elsewhere in the organization, we find an interesting response on the part of those who have discovered a capacity for leadership. They willingly subordinate themselves to a follower status and give way to the individual who is the most knowledgeable or better fit to lead an effort. The argument is that anyone can follow a leader, and that is perhaps true, but when leaders subordinate themselves it is with the absolute conviction that the individual who is the leader has commitment. The approach here is that true followership is the result of achieving the capacity to be a leader, and not before.

What does this mean to us in an organizational sense? How do we overcome the negative connotation of the word follower? We probably do not need to do so for those who understand the concept, but I would certainly hesitate to stand up in a room of fellow executives and state that I would desire them all to become followers. That statement would draw at least a few chuckles if not outrage. However, this is precisely the goal we should strive for within our organization, to move beyond leadership to followership. Perhaps we can sneak it in using a one-on-one technique of a mentor and protégée approach?

Mentorship

Not everyone can be a mentor, yet most of our organizations today seem to feel that it is a trait that is embedded in a position. We feel fairly casual about asking an individual to take on a mentorship task in the mistaken belief that they know fully the implication of such an assignment. In point of fact, the mentor is frequently selected by the protégée, and it is not unusual to see a mentorship relationship transcend organizational boundaries, although this may be threatening to the organization in a competitive sense.

A mentor who is not a follower may actually be doing more harm than good for the raising of leadership awareness in a protégée. The mentor is responsible for guiding the protégée through not only the administrative morass of the organization, but is also responsible for developing the managerial skills and leadership traits that are necessary for the individual to take a holistic view to benefit the organization while meeting individual needs. The mentor is a coach, yes. The mentor is also part teacher, part researcher, part friend, part disciplinarian, and even part student, for one of the great joys of mentoring is learning.

Some organizations have established a formal mentoring system and in some cases it is effective as a vehicle for training. We do have to start somewhere, and an imposed system is better than none at all. Organizations benefit when great care is made in selecting those to be assigned a mentor role and providing them with the training, education, tools, and resources to adequately accomplish their task of being a steward of the organization and to serve the objective of developing future leaders as part of the process.

Stewardship and Servant Leadership

In spite of the negative connotation associated with the terminology, when we examine the literal implementation of the concepts we are stunned by the accuracy and potential effectiveness of the approach suggested.

Stewardship can be applied across the entire organization, regardless of where we may find ourselves in the hierarchy. We are charged with the responsibility of applying assets to achieve a desired outcome, and the conservation of these assets, be they physical or human capital, is essential to produce the most cost effective outcome, or the most bang for the buck as the common saying advises. This conservation is stewardship.

Perhaps a less palatable word, but one that is actually more descriptive is that we serve the organization and must therefore subordinate our personal aspirations unless they are in consonance with the direction of the organization. This subordination of ego is very difficult to do, especially in results oriented individuals that tend to rise quickly in an organization. Yet we must be alert to remember that we are not engaged to gratify our egos but to encourage the best potential for the betterment of our organization. We can be very effective in encouraging our subordinates and peers to better performance.

Protégée

Being a protégée assumes responsibilities to the mentor as well as the organization and implies a willingness to subordinate, albeit temporarily, personal aspirations when deemed appropriate by the mentor to gain the breadth and depth of experience to succeed in the future. Loyalty toward the mentor and the organization is generally assumed and one enters the role of protégée with a clear understanding that it is a long term relationship that may transcend pure work related activities. It is not unusual to find a close affiliation between mentor and protégée so selection of a mentor must be approached with great care and the clear understanding that it is a mutual commitment.

A few words of explanation regarding placement of the protégée section after stewardship and servant leadership instead of directly after the mentorship section is in order. Although the relationship between mentor and protégée is so close that they should be treated together, we often find mentors assigned by an organization and it is not until the mentor becomes aware of the role in terms of stewardship and servant leadership that a true relationship with the protégée can be achieved. Protégées are frequently required to begin their learning assignments as members of a workgroup or a team, but more often as supervisors on a particular portion of a project or other short term undertaking that their mentor feels would be a good testing ground and one that will allow a good learning experience.

Supervise

Supervising skilled workers at a functional level or as a member of a project team is an interesting and demanding task that often allows us to exercise our abilities to think independently, albeit within established parameters, and to exercise our decision making capabilities. The task is not an easy one for we are frequently called upon to supervise the performance of highly skilled individuals with professional knowledge well beyond our own and to whom we may even appear to be incompetent. This is the main reason that functional level supervisors are usually those who have distinguished themselves in the field or profession and have achieved stature among their subordinates that is based on their professional competence.

As we begin to see frequent changes and increased technological flexibility in the workplace, we also see the knowledge gap lessening. Because of this decreasing power distance between supervisor and worker, we are increasingly finding this to be a good way to establish the people handling skills of a manager trainee, and to ensure that this trainee gets a firm grounding in the fundamental principles of the business. It is not unusual for a protégée to be moved among several functional areas to gain experience, and to broaden their awareness of the overall organization, before being placed in a position to learn managerial skills.

However convenient a training opportunity, we must never-the-less use great caution to not antagonize the workforce in the process. The supervisor is, after all, overhead and does not contribute directly to the revenue stream of the operation. When all concerned are clear that the supervisory assignment is for purposes of training, and that there is no intent to have the supervisor take on the trappings of an expert, can we justify placing anyone other than a well established professional who does indeed have the respect of the workers in the role.

Manage

Management theory has been around since Frederick Winslow Taylor introduced the principles of scientific management at the beginning of the 20th Century. In the 1980's we saw an explosion of prescriptive approaches that were replaced by systems thinking and organizational learning in the 1990's. We also saw the rise of project management to address one time efforts that had a definite start and stop date, consumed resources, and included high risk. By in large, it is the increase in risk and the globalization (Friedman, 1999) that brings such rapid and radical change as to increase the need for flatter and more responsive organizations.

The management discipline is under constant change and, as theory and practice come closer together in application, we see the emergence of a necessity for a continuous learning process

Tying it all together

It all boils down to people and keeping abreast of developments, not only in our chosen professions but across the broad spectrum of management and leadership theory as well as current events. We realize that we do not know everything and that each factual item contributes to acquiring a new perspective, and increased knowledge contributes to better quality decisions. Now let us investigate further

Management – Leadership Continuum

Managers and leaders in today's fast paced, highly competitive, multi-cultural, results oriented, operational environment must constantly strive to achieve a balance between tried and proven techniques and application of emerging technology, processes, and theories. To accomplish this, a balance between traditional management and leadership must be achieved. Defining these two terms is proving to be very elusive, and often contradictory. Perhaps we can best describe these terms, by applying definitions from several disciplines.

MANAGEMENT	←=========→	LEADERSHIP
Doing the 'thing' right	**Focus**	Doing the right 'thing'
Incremental	**Change**	Quantum
Directing	**Approach**	Encouraging
Adversarial	**Relationship**	Cooperative
Hierarchical	**Structure**	Matrix or Market Driven
Standardized	**Work**	Diverse and Creative
Production	**Orientation**	Process

Figure 2. The Management - Leadership Continuum

We have heard much in recent years of managers acting as 'change agents' within their sphere of responsibility. This guidance has been successfully applied in many companies, and the results are very clearly defined by several measures, chiefly cost reduction. In almost every case, success has been limited because of artificial constraints. We concentrate on accomplishing the defined task, but seldom permit ourselves to ask the crucial question of whether we should be doing the task at all. When acting as a manager then, we tend to apply tried and proven tools and techniques to accomplish the assigned task with the least expenditure of resources, because that is after all what managers are supposed to do; reduce the cost of production. Or, in non-profit and not-for-profit organizations, reduce the cost of providing the service. It is because we limit ourselves to reducing the use of the factors of production (Land, Labor, Capital, and Entrepreneurship), that change must be incremental for we cannot afford to take the risk of making quantum changes in the process. Yet it is the entrepreneur who operates with quantum change that is rewarded.

Historical Aspect of Management

Management theory for the past century has been oriented toward control of the production process, and our business schools have been very successful at producing managers skilled in directing the process as designed by engineers. We have considered the employee as an interchangeable part in the process. Perhaps that approach was justified in early production environments where less skill was required and the tasks were highly routinized. As labor unions came into ascendancy, the tasks themselves were incorporated into 'work rules' and the stage was set for an adversarial relationship. Encouragement for improving performance was often considered exploitative and managers relegated themselves to directing a standardized process in hierarchical organizational structures.

Because of this polarity between management at the one end and leadership at the other, it becomes clear that the successful manager of the future must also function as a leader. For the future, it becomes abundantly clear that we must possess the detail management skills and apply the

Shuhart Cycle of Plan-Do-Check-Act in order to continuously improve production or the service delivery processes. Therefore, implementation of such functions as total quality management, continuous process improvement, statistical process control, and other emerging applications designed to incrementally improve our processes remains a necessity.

At the opposite end of incremental change processes lies the quantum change domain, where we learn to question whether the process should be included at all. Here we use innovative techniques to eliminate redundant tasks, define new approaches to meeting our objectives, and make the hard decisions to abandon a process altogether. This domain is not easy to define, and it belongs predominantly to the entrepreneur and small startup company that typically has no previous experience in the process, although some attempt has been made by established firms to implement zero-basing, re-engineering, and other similar approaches. These are often confused for management techniques and because of that, we tend to set metrics using previous processes as a base, when the objective was to eliminate the process altogether. In the leadership domain we also follow a process whereby we envision the change desired, align the organization to accept the new technique, deploy the change, and learn from the results so that we can again envision a totally new process, or make a drastic shift and institute it as a process for incremental change.

What has become increasingly clear is the successful managers of the future must have the ability to be flexible and operate at several points along the management leadership continuum simultaneously. Being a manager will allow incremental change but will only succeed until a competitor makes a dramatic change that renders our process obsolete, or nearly so, and we lose market share or even succumb to annihilation. We also have dramatic evidence of new start-up companies that fail in a short period of time because their initial offering is superb and cannot be touched, but as soon as competitors adapt to the new environment, the start-up cannot move quickly enough to apply the necessary management techniques to reduce the costs and becomes non-competitive. To be responsive then, we must operate at both ends of the continuum as well as at several points along the scale as the operational need may dictate.

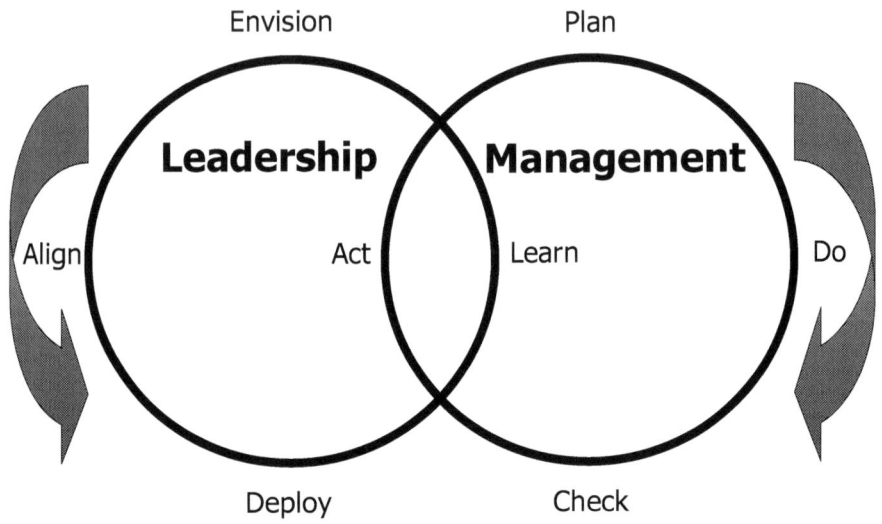

Carl Adams, 2000 – Adapted from Mantel & Meredith

Figure 3. The Leadership - Management Relationship

Current Application of Management Theory

As companies recognize the expanding business environment, and consumers grow more sophisticated, it is therefore no longer sufficient to make only incremental changes in our processes. Managers, supervisors, and individual workers must transition to leadership roles, and encourage subordinates and co-workers at the lowest level to take responsibility for their actions in maintaining the viability of the organization as a whole. This is often very difficult to do in a culture steeped in the adversarial labor-management relationship. Clearly, there exists a threat to the less skilled individual worker or supervisor, and improvements in processes will certainly lead to elimination of higher cost personnel who cannot, or will not, adapt to the rapidly changing environment. Yet this is the leadership dilemma existent in the work force today. How do we motivate employees, at all levels, to improve the processes and insure success of the organization in a highly competitive environment? In unionized work forces, the issue is even more critical. However, progressive unions are beginning to recognize that companies must be competitive to survive and cooperation, even in the face of a declining workforce, is better than losing all jobs to closure.

Highly successful firms have begun to recognize the need for situational application of a mix of management practice and leadership theory. They have taken steps to cross-train the work force to support matrix organizations, implemented informal lattice organizational structures based on mentorship, and made the effort to engage in the previously considered 'soft' factors of management to achieve better overall performance and greater responsiveness to external threats. Together with the application of technological advancements, a cooperative workforce can propel an organization into a successful competitive position.

The method for achieving an organization capable of remaining on the cutting edge of technology and implementation in a highly competitive environment is often elusive. Firms achieving the advantage tend to rest on their laurels until overcome by another. Why do these situations occur? Perhaps these situations occur as a lack of learning on the part of the organization. If we accept that organizations, as a whole, can indeed learn and function as single entities, then we can take steps to ensure long term viability. This takes vision, understanding, and an ability to tolerate risk. The work of Chris Argyris, spanning several decades, clearly illustrates that organizations can indeed learn, and when the managers in the organization become leaders and assume risk, the results can be significant. Argyris in *Knowledge for Action* published by Josey-Bass in 1993 touches on the definitions we are investigating:

> "There are at least two types of organizational learning. One focuses on changing organizational routines. It is incremental and adaptive. The second focuses on practices that lead to a new framework for learning and to new routines." (Knowledge for Action, p. xii)

The adaptive manager then must keep current in the actionable research in the field, and be prepared to adapt new techniques to the existing processes. The adaptive leader must broaden the horizon, conduct inquiry beyond the industry in which the organization is positioned, and seek to adapt actionable academic research as well as borrow from other fields as appropriate. The horizon is broad indeed and an inquiring mind is crucial to success.

Planning for Leadership

Now that we see leadership is desirable as a concurrent mix with management, and that people are the key to success, we must look at how to achieve this management-leadership balance in the future. The literature on human capital as well as satisfaction and turnover is very rich and allows us a view of the myriad possibilities. However, Noel Tichey has made some interesting observations regarding the time investment required to achieve organization leadership hierarchy.

Investment in the human capital of the organization is often termed empowerment, but must be practiced with great care. The culture of the organization must change in consonance with the empowerment strategy, and the process must be carefully monitored to ensure that the direction of development is in keeping with the goals of the organization. A careful approach consisting of all methods of human development is called for.

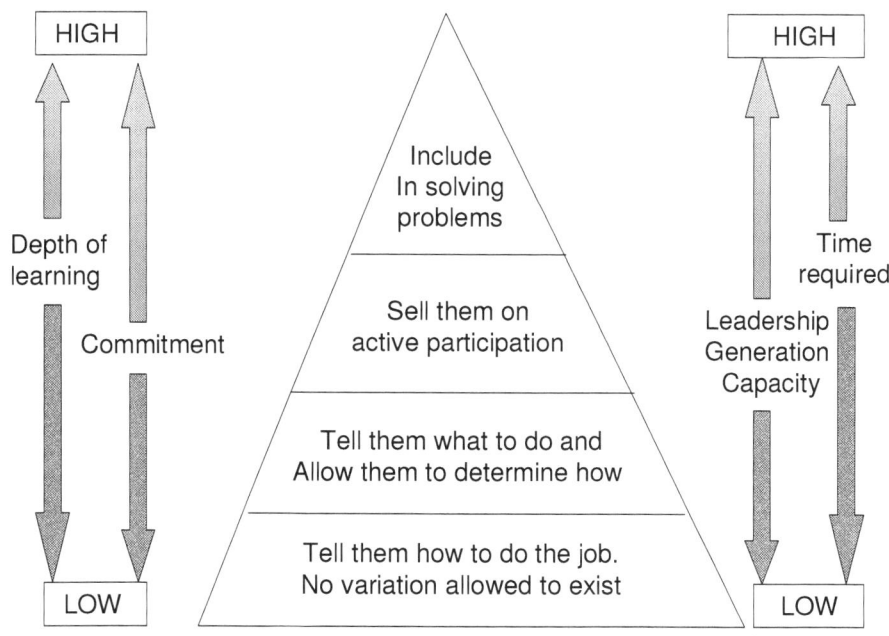

Adapted from Noel Tichey *The Leadership Engine*

Figure 4. Creating Future Leaders Takes Time and Effort

Although rather obvious, the need to enter into a long range education program to develop leaders is often overlooked in favor of short term training programs that promise quick results. The success of mentor-protégé programs point out that successful education of leaders is a combination of education, training, and on the job performance. The chief drawback is the amount of time and resources required to produce an adequate depth of leaders for the future. If not in place, the prompt start of such a program is clearly required at all levels of the organization. However, it is interesting to note that although the investment in time, when properly planned, generates increased learning as well as commitment to the organization and, as the organization progresses from being top down driven to participatory, the quality and number of potential leaders increases.

The Bottom Line

The key however, is always people. People, like ropes, can be pulled successfully, but pushing people has the same effect as pushing a rope. The skilled executive, supervisor, project manager, or enlightened worker will know when to apply the requisite pressure to accomplish a specific task and when to stop and listen to others more knowledgeable. We frequently forget that the person who knows the most about the task is the skilled worker performing the work. As challenges to meeting cost and schedule appear, it is generally incumbent on the manager to exercise a little leadership and solicit alternatives from the real experts, the ones performing the tasks. However, the groundwork must be done well prior to the need in order to maintain creditability. This is where the mix between leadership and management becomes an issue. Plan ahead.

Organizational Learning

So far we have attempted to define management and leadership as they apply in general terms but these tools set the stage for investigating organizational structures which best support a cooperative and effective prosecution of a project, strategy, or business policy. We sometimes fail to notice that we may have several organizational structures in place concurrently and that wide gaps may exist between the formal structure as shown on carefully prepared organizational charts and the reality of the informal structure that dominates our day to day organizational activities. When we understand the structures available, their strengths and weaknesses, and their reception by segments within our organization, we can effectively apply them in both a formal and informal context to attain the best mix for the benefit of ourselves as well as the organization.

Organizational Structure

The traditional separation between management and labor has been the empowerment to make decisions or direct the accomplishment of work in a particular manner. Going a step further, the separation between managers and executives has been in the scope of the decisions, with executives making commitments that bind the company contractually. We are generally aware of the historical and some emerging organizational structure from our personal experiences. We often feel that we must conform to the organizational structure dictated by organizational charts or the desires of our supervisors, and that is very true in a formal sense. However, we have infinite control over our informal structures. We know for example that although the Mayor or City Manager makes the decision in the town where we live, getting the information to the decision maker is dependent on the administrative assistant. If we are to influence the decision process, we have learned that getting the information we would like to place before the decision maker must be in a form that is acceptable to several staff members. We therefore note the formal organization, but then informally discover that the agenda for the administrative assistant is heavily skewed by campaign contributions so we gain access by making a contribution. Is this any way to do business? Of course, and we have been doing so for decades. The key is to understand the formal and informal structures that are in place and take advantage of each to gain the knowledge that will make our organization and ourselves more competitive for the future. To assist us in understanding organizational structures we can look at history to assist us.

Organization of the Clan

The clan is probably the oldest organizational structure, and this type of organization is still seen today, albeit on an informal basis, in several cultures. This is simply a banding of individuals, or families, in a loose organization where each individual has a voice in the management of the group. There are no specific barriers to entry or departure from the group and members may enter or leave, as they desire, although entering the group may be subject to approval of the membership. The chief discriminator is one of relationships where each member of the group interacts with every other member of the group and decision-making is clearly an individual effort. Situational leaders may emerge, and the group may choose to follow their decisions or reject them without censure by the group. More applicable to small groups of individuals, it nonetheless has been applied to rather large informal structures in Chinese culture under the broad term of guanxi (Cheng, 1997). Today a clan type of organization is seen in cooperatives of various sorts, and in the emerging discipline of networking. Although networking tends to serve as an informal means of communication among peers, considerable networking takes place among small business owners in particular locales that tend to patronize each other for their business needs. In its larger and more diversified mode where a patriarch or matriarch type of leader emerges, the organization may take on a blending of the clan organization with that of a dynastic leader (Weidenbaum, 1998). With the emergence of a single leader, the stage is set for a fiefdom.

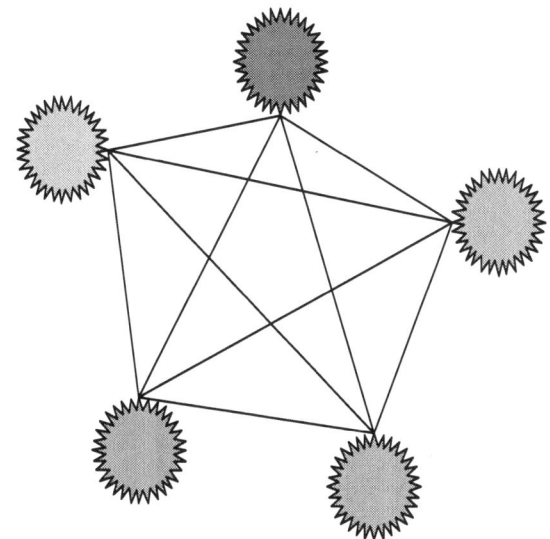

Figure 5. Clan Structure

Fiefdom

History is replete with examples of a single leader guiding all activities:

- Lord of an estate in Medieval England with one or several villages under his charge
- European kingdoms

- Most dictatorships
- Pre World War II Japan
- Today in North Korea and several third world nations
- Small businesses and sole proprietorships
- Many fraternal and social organizations

What each of these organizations has in common is that a single leader provides the guidance for all activities and is the sole arbiter of propriety. The span of control in each case is absolute within the domain, regardless of the method of acquisition. An argument can be made for a benign versus a hostile role on the part of the leader, but regardless of philosophy, the absolute power of the individual drives the conduct of all activities and each transaction must conform to the desires of that individual.

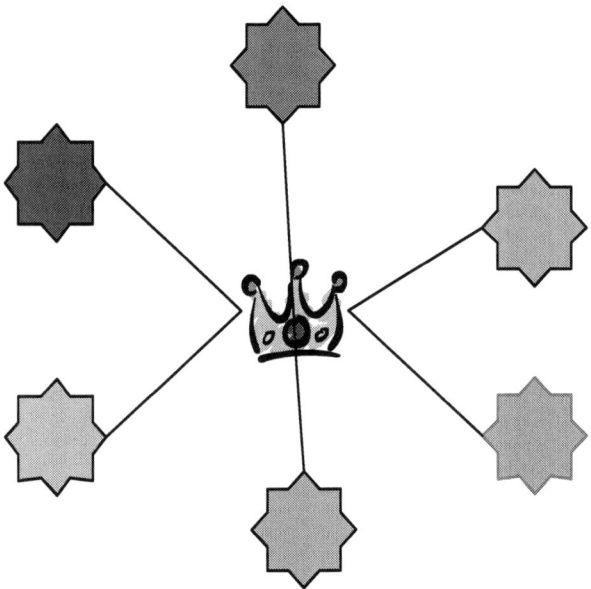

Figure 6. Fiefdom has a single strong leader

Since individual desires tend to change over time, the change is seldom open to dialogue and often implemented abruptly. Conducting business in such an environment is perilous unless you are the one in charge. International projects may include operations in nations with this type of structure, or may draw labor from countries with this type of government. In the business world, most sole proprietorships operate in this manner, at least during their growth period, although an argument can be made that in small business employees do have the alternative of leaving their employment and are therefore not tied to the business owner. The advantage of dealing with this type of organization is the ease of obtaining a determination and consequently a commitment. The difficulty with this type of organization is that as it grows in size, the span of personal control becomes eroded and authority is delegated to trusted subordinates who exercise considerable control within their own domains, often without accountability, as long as the desired outcomes are obtained. Of interest is that this type of organization is quite often seen in both for-profit and non-profit organizations as an informal structure.

We will see the informal manifestation of fiefdoms more often in the public sector as individuals build 'empires' to enhance their own position within a formal hierarchical structure.

Hierarchical Structure

Bureaucracies form when the organization becomes large and no single individual can effectively control its operations. Typically authority is delegated to subordinates who will exercise considerable power in their sphere of influence. The organizational structure is well defined and rules governing its operation proliferate. This type of organization tends to compartmentize functions and often the biggest problem associated with obtaining a determination is finding the appropriate person within the structure with the authority to make the decision. Although many bureaucracies are associated with government entities, and these are predominantly the bureaucracies that first come to mind as those we may have to deal with, nonetheless a significant number of bureaucracies exist at varying levels of complexity in industry and the non-profit sector as well. In every case however, the organization is structured around functional requirements.

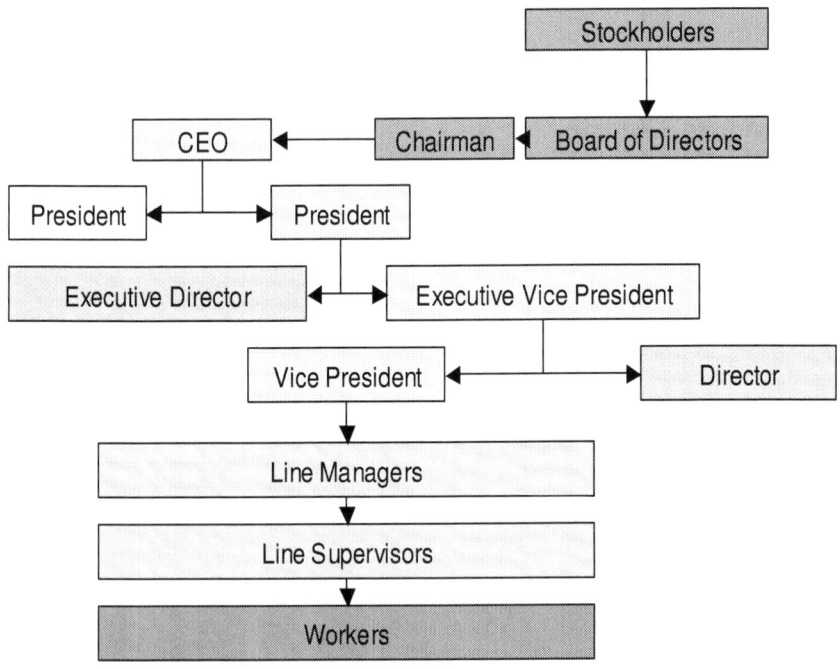

Figure 7. A Typical Hierarchical Structure

A distinction must be made between North American and European titles. In the United States, Directors are typically staff designations, while in Europe they may be line positions. In complex structures, the shareholders elect the Board of

Directors who selects a Chairman. The Board of Directors hires the Chief Executive Officer and the CEO then fills the organization. In the diagram shown here, the executive line organization stops at the office of a Vice President and the management organization continues. This top-heavy organizational structure still exists in large corporations where the need is driven by the diversity of operations or the geographic dispersal of activity, but is largely giving way to flatter structures more responsive to customer requirements.

Market Driven Organization Structures

This market driven organization category is rather broad, and may be both diverse and confusing since it encompasses not only the semi-traditional adaptation of consumer driven supply and demand schedule, but also includes many emerging structures, tailored by market demands.

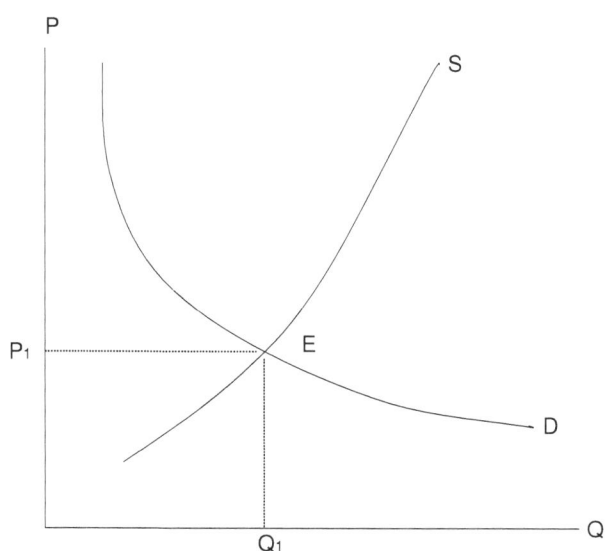

Figure 8. Classic Supply and Demand Schedule

The ability to maximize profit for the organization, and operate as close to equilibrium (shown as 'E' in Figure 8) as possible is the goal of every manager. Since economics teaches us that the market controls the price, managers have been charged to reduce costs in order to maximize profit. In order to accomplish this in today's rapidly evolving, technology driven economy, highly competitive companies have created hybrid organizational structures to accommodate the demands of the market.

Here we find very specific organizations described as distribution channels as well as the matrix organization becoming more common in project management and intellectual driven endeavors. Of note is the opportunity for empowerment and situational leadership at all levels of the organization, especially when market forces are understood across the entire organizational structure. The key to successful implementation is in adopting a systems approach that takes into consideration many issues including economics, market factors, internal capabilities, and the customer, along with a plethora of others, which may be undergoing rapid change.

Distribution Channels

We will not dwell on this area except to point out the technology drivers responsible for the emergence of this type of organization. As communications channels became more reliable and the use of computer based technology became readily available, companies involved in the distribution of systems and components from multiple manufacturers to customers began to eliminate middle and upper management in favor of empowering their line operators who also act as the sales staff and order takers. This necessitated a change from semi-skilled order takers to highly trained and very knowledgeable individuals who not only take orders but are able to guide the customer in the proper selection of the products required to fill the customer's needs. Orders are then sent to fulfillment centers across the world where the order is assembled and shipped to the customer. This process would not have been possible even a decade ago and only taking advantage of emerging technology made it possible. Today the process is being further streamlined by the consumer assembling the components directly on a web site and submitting the order directly to the fulfillment center. Again, technology is making these cost savings possible. This is an example of the computer industry, but the same concept applies across many other fields.

Matrix Organization

Emerging as the organization of choice for managing well-educated, highly skilled, individuals is the matrix organization. This structure has been embraced by project managers and their more knowledgeable sponsors within organizations large and small. This structure permits the application of required labor only at the time and for the duration necessary to complete specified tasks as determined by the project manager. The labor comes from a pool of individuals within a functional area headed by a functional manager who is responsible for

- Providing the qualified individuals
- Training of the individuals in functional skills
- Performance of the project task
- Quality of the project task
- Delivery within acceptable parameters of time and budget

This organizational structure frees the functional manager to concentrate on the area of expertise associated with the functional area and allows the project manager to interface among the several functional managers to ensure that the requirements of the project

- Proceed at an optimum pace
- Stay within budget
- Meet customer requirements
- Meet company objectives
- Satisfy the customer

These tried and true project management objectives have undergone a subtle change in the last few years with:

- Delivery at a mutually agreeable time
- Under the established budget
- Exceed the customer requirements where feasible
- Surpass the company objectives
- Delight the customer

The key to an organization of this type is communication, and once again, the people. However, even in a dynamic organizational structure where all are empowered to take necessary action to meet the objectives and modify the strategies as necessary to deliver the highest quality product, we find difficulties because of the semi-rigid structure and defined roles that may limit individual initiative.

Lattice Organization

Lattice Organization is a newer movement that emerges from the perceived short falls of matrix organizations. It is usually established among a few individuals within a larger organizational structure, normally among executives and senior managers initially. The lattice structure can be successfully driven down as the organization embraces a systems approach and organizational learning. This structure is not new however, and has been in use since ancient times when we saw it on a much smaller and more formalized scale with a master and his apprentice. Today we use the terms mentor, or coach, and protégée, but essentially it is still one individual taking responsibility for the professional development of another. In a learning organization we recognize that human capital is important and do not place limitations in a formal sense. This position allows a mentor to take a protégé under their wing. The protégé is also free to provide guidance to another within, or indeed outside, the organization. The influence on the mentor is from above, from the protégé, as well as peers horizontally. Of interest in a lattice structure is that the protégé may take guidance, and receive support, from several superiors. This type of less formal organizational structure exists in systems driven companies, small start-up operations, and most non-profit and not-for-profit organizations at a local level.

Additional Thoughts on Organizations

As we proceed to areas of practice, it is important to understand that no single prescriptive approach will work for all organizations. Effective leaders and good managers take what is applicable from each successful implementation that fits their own needs at the time, for implementation, discarding those features which do not apply, and modify others to suit their individual needs. We are often constrained by the organizational structure imposed on us by the hierarchy, but may have considerable latitude to implement a demand structure of our own choosing at a local or group level, providing we do not circumvent the mandatory reporting process, and take into consideration all factors of the system we work within.

Leadership Practice

In practice, application of leadership and management skills within an organization are largely at the sufferance of upper level management. As individuals we are constantly torn between demands from a plethora of sources:

- Those above us in the organization who will establish the pattern for acceptable behavior.
- Our peers within the organization who will ensure that we do not exercise our ingenuity in unacceptable ways.
- Our subordinates who place a responsibility on us to behave ourselves and conduct our business in an acceptable manner.
- Our customers who expect acceptable performance and will reward us for compliance and punish us for unacceptable behavior.
- End users of our products who will vote with their purchasing power.
- Service providers who can actively support our efforts or place a burden on our ability to be effective.
- Suppliers who can make inbound logistics a challenge.
- Distributors who may assist us by placing a priority on our products and services.
- Family obligations that can detract from the full commitment of our employees.
- Social obligations that may adversely impact our ability to perform at a superior level.
- Unsolicited intrusions on our time that can adversely impact our individual productivity.

Dance of Blind Reflex

Our response to each of these demands is situational, and the priorities we set for our response is frequently based on our perception of security. Mostly we engage in what Barry Oshry (Oshry, 1995) refers to as the "Dance of Blind Reflex" or "DBR" where we do what is the obvious and expected in order to move the issue aside so we can proceed with what we perceive as being the real need. Over the past two decades executives, managers, and supervisors have been inundated with devices and strategies for time management, prioritizing, and other mechanical aides to increase our effectiveness in a highly complex and very organized world. None of these however address the real issue of problem solving by reducing the complexity of the process.

Margaret Wheatley in *Leadership and the New Science* as well in her *A Simpler Way* suggests that we tend to seek out the more complex solution because it appears to be more elegant and must be better. Wheatley suggests that relying on a simpler approach would produce better results in the long term. Peter Senge also voiced this sentiment in his presentation to the Practitioner Series at the Academy of Management in San Diego, California in August 1998. Senge suggested that many of today's problems are the result of yesterday's solutions. The thread in each case is DBR, the dance of blind reflex. We continue to fix the symptom rather than the cause.

In *Lessons From The New Workplace*, a video from CRM Films, L.P., Wheatley's principles are implemented in three rather diverse organizations; the U.S. Army, Dupont Corporation, and a North Carolina School System. Of specific interest is a prescriptive approach to problem solving using three broad categories; information, relationships, and vision.

Information
- What information do I need?
- What information do I have?
- What restricts the flow?

Relationships
- What are our formal relationships?
- What are our real relationships?
- Is there agreement/discord between them?

Vision
- Do we have a shared purpose?
- Do we work from it?
- How do we know?

The film shows what can be accomplished by a thorough analysis of each event, whether success or a failure. The key here is that each decision-making event must be analyzed for optimum success. If we only analyze failures we will never learn whether our successes could have been greater. The U.S. Army has instituted this in the form of an After Action Report (AAR) and closely parallels what is generally known in industry as a 'lessons learned' summary. Wheatley provides us three questions to ask after each event:

1. What happened?
2. Why do we think it happened?
3. What can we learn from it?

To which we could add

4. Where do we go from here?

Implications for Managers

What are the implications for managers from all these studies?

More and more we are finding a blending of academic rigor and practitioner pragmatism. Scholarly journals continue to focus more on applied research and are actively soliciting collaborative research for publication. Even the Academy of Management (http://aom.pace.edu/), long known for its rigorous academic treatment of management theory, has embarked on an effort to include practitioners in its activities, including the formation of a Practitioner Series Interest Group in 1999, the first step toward establishing a recognized track.

Why this interest?

Managers, in their transition to situational leaders, must obtain information from all sources available. Unfortunately the creditability of many sources of information, especially many of the readily available on-line references, is highly suspect. Investigations carried out with academic rigor are usually creditable, and after passing peer review, become a reliable source of information for the practitioner. It is this access to creditable and reliable information which most professional societies are attempting to provide. Nothing however, is entirely free.

Leader-managers in the future will have to participate in the information process by sharing. Membership in at least one professional society, or organization, will become mandatory and we must expect to devote the necessary time to ensure that the source of information remains current and useful. We should expect our organization to understand that to gain the maximum benefit from membership, we as individuals should:

- Attend local chapter meetings
- Read the journal
- Attend the annual meeting
- Contribute articles for presentation and publication

Another useful feature of attending local, national, and international professional society meeting is to take advantage of networking opportunities. Frequently emerging technology is discussed informally, and an opportunity is afforded to speak directly with those involved in the implementation process.

The key is to take advantage of every opportunity to learn. Learn to question. And then diffuse the information throughout the organization so all can take advantage of the knowledge.

Systems Thinking

Although difficult to understand the formalized style of Bertalanffy (Bertalanffy, 1969), his seminal work on systems theory is well worth the effort for anyone who wishes to get a better understanding of the foundation of the discipline that has become known as systems theory. Bertalanffy (1969) relies on his biologic and physics background to compare living organisms and their interdependence with their environment. Although he alludes to both open and closed systems, our main concern is with open systems because these more closely approximate the conditions in the operating environment for business and non-profit organizations alike. His 1969 work was embraced by business and management academicians who saw in it the foundation for explaining the complex interrelationships we see in the ever increasing pace of global business. However, his work was difficult to introduce into the undergraduate program due to its complexity and trans-disciplinary approach, so it did not get the exposure to future business leaders in a way that was effective.

To better understand the issues involved, and to clarify the application of the theory to practice in the real world, Checkland introduced it in a more readable and acceptable form for use at the university level and as a consequence, many well-educated industry leaders received their introduction to a holistic approach in a more formalized manner (Checkland, 1993). He continued his work in this area and reduced the thirty years of research to a summary that any student of systems thinking should be aware of (Checkland, 1999). Fortunately Checkland was not alone in the pursuit of knowledge in this area and we see several differing perspectives in application and more readable versions (Capra, 1996) can be found that together with the seminal work establishes a foundation that is difficult to ignore.

Table 1. Matrix of Peter Senge's Five Disciplines

	PRACTICES What we do	PRINCIPLES Guiding ideas and insights	ESSENCES State of being when mastered
Personal Mastery	Clarify personal vision Holding creative tension Make choices	Vision Creative vs. emotional tension Subconscious	Being Generativeness Connectedness
Mental Models	Distinguish experience from generalization Test assumptions Left hand column	Espoused theory vs. theory in use Ladder of inference Balance inquiry and advocacy	Love of truth Openness
Shared Vision	Acknowledge current reality Visioning process (sharing, listening, choice)	Shared vision as hologram Commitment vs. compliance	Common purpose Partnership
Team Learning	Suspend assumptions Act as colleagues Surface own defensiveness Practice	Dialogue Integrate dialogue Defensive routines	Collective Intelligence Alignment
Systems Thinking	Archetypes Simulation	Structure influences behavior Policy resistance Leverage	Holism Inter-connectedness

Adapted from: Senge, Peter (1990) The Fifth Discipline, Doubleday

Peter Senge, author of *The Fifth Discipline: The Art and Practice of Learning Organizations* (Senge, 1990), and one of the principle researchers on learning organizations and systems thinking, suggests that no single approach to managerial problem solving is acceptable in the long term. He has stated (Academy of Management, Practitioner Series, San Diego, 1998) that 'today's problems are a result of yesterday's solutions.' The implication is that in most cases, managers tend to address the symptom instead of the underlying issues driving the undesirable effect.

These five disciplines are fully developed in *The Fifth Discipline: The Art and Practice of Learning Organizations* (Senge, 1990) and *The Fifth Discipline Fieldbook* (Senge, 1994), and are expanded in the form of sustaining the growth process of profound change in *The Dance of Change* (Senge et al., 1999). A matrix of these five disciplines in terms of practices, principles, and essences was adapted from Appendix I of *The Fifth Discipline: The Art and Practice of Learning Organizations* (1990) and may be of help in following the discussion. In addition, independent work by Brian Oshry in *Seeing Systems* (Oshry, 1995) provides a clear view of the differing perceptions among uppers, middles, and lowers within organizations and the perception of customers from without the organizational structure.

Personal Mastery

Senge suggests that one must first achieve the essence of **personal mastery** or a balance of core personal vision and the reality of their current personal environment. Although this seems intuitive, it is clear that without knowing ourselves as individuals first, we cannot make the distinction between our own aggrandizement and the needs of our firm, company, institution, or other environment. He holds that we are constantly being pulled between alternatives and making choices is a part of life. And, with a clear personal vision we tend to make decisions subconsciously that are in consonance with our core beliefs. Without a clear personal vision, we tend to lose our direction.

Understanding ourselves is not as easy as it may seem. However, we can take advantage of a retrospective where we examine our past attitudes and actions and attempt to relate them to the environment in which we made the decision. We can also take advantage of the several personal inventory tools that are available to us at little or no cost. With the advent of the Internet, many of these tools are available online and, although they are free only because the data is generally aggregated by the owner of the web site for marketing purposes, the instruments do provide us with information we can use. Alternately, many universities include personal assessment instruments as part of the curriculum in both undergraduate and graduate courses, and we can even contact our local community college to take advantage of low cost options.

Taking advantage of the measurement tools is but one part of the process and we must continue to evaluate the results in light of our personal knowledge. The results are usually more of a predictor than an indicator, and given the conditions can change over time. It is the change that we are interested in, and that takes introspection. The time spent in reflection and getting to know ourselves is well worth the effort, even if we do find out things about ourselves that we would rather were not true.

An example of undesirable personal findings is to uncover our prejudice for or against an issue. This is not at all unusual and we all have our prejudices, perhaps formed very early in our lives, and some of later origin. Prejudices are simply a perception that may or may not be true, and may even be deemed unacceptable in the society in which we function. However, if we can identify the prejudice, we can guard against it serving as an influence in our decision making.

Of course we continue to grow in intellect and are modified by our life experiences as we live longer, so we should take the time to reflect on ourselves from time to time in order to update our self knowledge. Senge refers to this process as self mastery for the excellent reason that we must know ourselves thoroughly to accept where we are, and where we are is constantly changing. Personal mastery is therefore an ongoing process and not an event. When we know ourselves, it allows us the opportunity to better determine our position regarding the plethora of issues we deal with on a daily basis. We must delve deeply into ourselves before we can understand how we interact with the external environment.

Mental Models

Our environment, including the constraints placed by law, regulation, customs and traditions, personal values, and expectations of our associates, largely forms our actions and behaviors. Our attitudes and perceptions form an internal view of the environment. These are categorized as **mental models**, and form the second discipline as described by Senge. The essence of this discipline is openness and the pursuit of truth.

We often take the easy way in only looking for evidence that supports our preconceived ideas, largely because we have been trained in our education system to establish a hypothesis and then to seek evidence to support it. However, life is very messy. We should find evidence to both challenge and support our theses, premises, or suppositions and none should be ignored as each contributes something to our better understanding of the overall issue. It is very comfortable to find agreement, but it is the challenge that allows us to grow.

Developing a mental model of truth and openness is difficult because we must continue to operate in an environment where this approach is not always considered to be desirable. Forming a mental model that allows one to examine every available facet of an issue and allows mistakes as a learning experience is often unacceptable to our associates, yet is a powerful tool when properly used in a balanced approach.

Shared Vision

Since we do not function independently, we tend to seek out organizations, and share activities, that are based on similar values, or share like interests. These same personal constraints exist in the business or organizational environment but we seldom have the opportunity to select our associates in these cases. However, this is not a deterrent to achieving a **shared vision** to enter into a partnership within the organization and to achieve a common purpose.

We can begin the process independently but because we function in an organization we must share our knowledge, attitudes, and ideas with others to be successful. Not an easy task as we will generally find that our colleagues and associates are at differing levels of personal mastery, and some have no clear mental model of themselves or their interaction with the environment in which we operate.

Nothing sets a better example than success and when we are confident in ourselves and have a clear established direction, we tend to exhibit the characteristics that others wish to emulate. Because we have a clear direction in mind, it becomes easier for us to communicate this direction to our colleagues and associates and solicit their commitment. Of course we do not always obtain commitment initially and will have to settle for participation, or what is termed 'buy-in' where the associate does not opt to share in the responsibility for success as in commitment. But as more individuals in the organization learn and form mental models, commitment becomes easier to obtain and the sharing of information on a team level becomes a viable approach.

Team Learning

We must learn to suspend our assumptions and engage in dialogue to achieve a collective objective. This is often very difficult for it requires a suspension of our defensive routines and even exposure of our vulnerability in confidence that our colleagues will not violate our trust. Only through open dialogue is it possible to align our several individual agendas to achieve a collective goal. With mutual trust, **team learning** is achievable.

In this phase we rely more on the members of our organization having achieved the previous steps of the process for it is very difficult to open oneself to vulnerability without some assurance that our trust is not misplaced. This trust must extend beyond the immediate group of associates and colleagues to the organization as a whole, but we must be secure in our own mind that our openness will not be turned against us to threaten our personal security. We saw earlier in our discussion of Margaret Wheatley's work that we must learn from each event, but the learning can only take place in an atmosphere of openness and trust. Imagine analyzing an event when what happened, returns a collective assessment of failure. Would you be able to state under why do we think it happened that an action on your part contributed to it? This takes a level of trust that must be present for only then can we continue to what we can learn from it and where do we go from here.

The strength of team learning is that we are able to marshal our best resources to address any emergent issue and when we share our experiences we become stronger and more able to meet the emergent demands of future challenges by application of a trans-disciplinary, holistic, approach.

Systems Thinking

When alignment within the organization is achieved, it becomes easier to see the factors acting upon the organization. These factors are both positive and negative, but each affects the functionality of the organization, and perhaps continued viability as well. The structure of the organization must be changed to accommodate the learning organization in order to allow each participant to develop fully. Only then is a holistic approach possible. This fifth discipline is **system thinking**.

The key to achieving a learning organization that embraces the principles of a systems approach to understanding and problem solving is to allow each individual to function in an atmosphere where reflection is encouraged, trust is valued, and errors in judgment tolerated and examined for lessons learned for future application. Not an easy task, especially in public organizations that must post quarterly profits that are at least equal to market in order to raise operating capital and satisfy stockholders. Yet this is exactly what must be accomplished in order to build an organization that is responsive to change.

Implementing a Systems Approach

In practice, these disciplines are very difficult to implement and considerable effort must be put forth across all levels of the organization in order to achieve success. That success is possible has been demonstrated in *The Fifth Discipline Fieldbook* (1994) and again in *The Dance of Change* (1999). Each suggests that the implementation requires considerable organizational commitment.

- Why are major companies queuing up to obtain the services of Peter Senge and his group at the Massachusetts Institute of Technology to assist in the implementation process?

- Why are companies willing to divert resources from production to perhaps achieve an ethereal advantage?

- Why are companies willing to make a long-term commitment to a process that the authors and implementers acknowledge is transitory and will require firm commitment to sustain?

Visionaries are predicting ever increasing competition in a global marketplace for organizations engaged in virtually all areas of endeavor. These predictions include:

- Increased commitment to excellence in quality
- Increased levels of service
- Customization of previously considered standard products
- Commitment to on-time delivery performance
- Concern for environmental issues
- And the list goes on

Organizations that will be able to compete in fast paced, highly competitive environments are those, which have established a vision and managed to successfully communicate it across all levels of the organization. When coupled with empowerment of employees to make decisions based on the situation, it allows the organization to function in consonance with the vision without direct involvement of upper management in the decision process. These attributes can be enhanced when the five disciplines are implemented and a level of trust exists, not only within the organization, but also between the organization and its customers and suppliers. And, when the essences of the five disciplines are achieved, and reinforced, the basis for a learning organization is in place, allowing synergy in dealings with internal and external entities. Again, people are the key to success, but an educated and committed leadership is necessary for sustained development.

In implementing a systems approach in learning organizations, it is sometimes difficult to remember that this is a process that must be implemented over time and, as we near our goals, we find that we must begin anew because our perspective changes. We have often heard that the only constant is change, and in this case at least the statement can be relied on absolutely. In order to achieve a holistic approach and a dedicated and committed learning organization we must be willing to embrace change as a necessary and desirable part of the overall process.

Barry Oshry's View

Barry Oshry (Oshry, 1995) presents a non-academic view of systems thinking, primarily from his experience in conducting workshops for corporate executives. The thrust here is that there must be clear lines of communication, not only in the traditional fashion, but interactively throughout the entire organization and its customers. He stresses a clear line between each member of the organization and the customer and avoidance of doing business as usual, or performing the "Dance of Blind Reflex" (DBR). He provides a look at the individual in an unfolding drama:

Figure 9. Many forces act on us

We like to believe that we have some control over our environment, but when the stress of operations takes over we find that we have varying degrees of control as an event unfolds. We may have some control over our suppliers, but in a competitive environment our suppliers are generally free to seek their business where their costs are reduced. Suppliers are not willing to engage in personalized service unless there is a clear requirement to do so, and it results in an increased profit. In practice, at some critical point we feel that we are controlled by our suppliers and this leads to stress and frustration.

Our colleagues and associates have their own responsibilities and, in spite of the customary approach that we are in an organization to assist each other for the betterment of the organization as a whole, there is usually little doubt that in a real world, the cooperative spirit is only operative when there is a clear benefit to those involved. This negotiation takes time and always seems to be required at a period when time is a crucial commodity.

Even our subordinates have certain expectation of our behavior and may wish to exercise their desires to approach performance differently than one would like. Depending on the level of holistic thinking in an organization, some move toward autonomy may actually be desirable, but is difficult to accept initially. Interesting to note is that as leadership emerges at lower levels of the organization this is the area where we begin to see it manifest itself as individuals uncover better ways to execute routine tasks. A learning organization would welcome such an initiative.

Distributors look upon you as a supplier of their goods and services and as you attempt to deliver to your schedule, they will be demanding their own schedule take priority. I believe we just covered the process from the other end? It is always difficult to place ourselves in the other person's shoes, but we must do so if we are to achieve a systems view.

There is no substitute for the demands of the customer for they are, after all, the determining reason for our continued existence and we ignore customer demands at our peril. Clearly, the customer is the driving force and Oshry brings this point home by emphasizing that the organization will function best when every individual has a clear view of customer needs and acts accordingly. Pretty strong approach but one that has proven to be true in a very practical sense as more and more customers are becoming knowledgeable and begin to see alternative means to satisfy their needs.

Our superiors want to ensure that we are in full compliance with their wishes for they, after all, are the ones who are responsible to the stockholders, board of directors, or fill in whatever blank you wish. The amount of pressure they can exert is vast and can be threatening, unless the learning organization has advanced systems thinking to the executive level.

The key here is that regardless of whether the individual is an upper, middle, or a bottom; there are actions that seem threatening to the individual. Oshry further categorizes the organization as being composed of individuals with the perspectives shown in Table 2.

Table 2. Oshry's Table of Values

	Environment	Survival Process	Overlooked Process	Relationship Breakdown
Top	Complexity & Responsibility	Differentiation	Differentiation Integration	Turf
Middle	Diffusion	Individuation	Integration	Alienation
Bottom	Shared Vulnerability	Integration	Individuation Differentiation	GroupThink

We see from the work conducted by Barry Oshry that we must acknowledge each broad group of individuals on the basis of their perceived environment and to consider their impact on the organization.

Environmental Impact

Looking at the environment alone we see that there is a vast difference between top and bottom in the organization. The uppers deal with complex trans-disciplinary issues while the lowers tend to feel that they share vulnerability to actions

51

made at levels where they have no input. We can see that in a traditional organization the level of responsibility, although inherent at each level for the specific task or process, varies its impact on the organization as a whole in direct proportion to the position. Those at the bottom are charged with the responsibility of ensuring that their work is performed to at least minimum expectations, but hopefully exceed them. Those at the top are charged with broader responsibilities but are dependent on their subordinates for the conversion of their vision to reality. Those in the middle of the organization, the supervisors and managers, have either achieved their peak of responsibility or are actively seeking promotion and additional responsibility so have much different needs.

Approaches to Ensure Survival

The uppers tend to seek differentiation as each is motivated to excel above their competitors for higher position in the organization on the basis of their unique problem solving skills. Since executives rise and fall on their decision making processes, and the quality of their decisions are what is considered, this group seeks to gain additional knowledge through education, activities in professional societies, performing research in related areas, and engaging in a broad reading program to enhance their decision making capability. The middles survive by showing individual strength in their particular field and attempt to hoard the knowledge that will make them vulnerable. Those seeking upward mobility in the organization will usually embark on a course of study by seeking advanced degrees, and otherwise begin to emulate the uppers approach to expanding their knowledge. While some lowers will also attempt to increase their knowledge in preparation for advancement, most will seek protection by integration into a collective bargaining group or association to collectively protect their positions, often on the basis of seniority rather than performance.

Overlooked Processes of Survival

While differentiation continues to be a major driver with uppers, some integration does take place as professional societies begin to lend more support for networking opportunities and informal alliances are formed on the strength of individual contributions to the professional society. As the trappings of a learning organization begin to emerge and a systems approach is accepted across much of the organization, it is not unusual to begin to see some integration with both middles and lowers in the organization that have the ability to contribute to the overall success of the organization. It is this drive for integration that is often overlooked and must be addressed to achieve success.

Breakdown of Relationships

The outward appearance of a relationship breakdown is generally first seen in turf wars being fought among upper management, and perhaps even an attempt to actively involve subordinates, which can quickly lead to alienation among the middles and the joining of lowers to solidify their position within the organization as a protective measure. The lowers begin to act and think alike and will withdraw their individual and collective support, in favor of a safer course of action in doing what they are told.

Additional Thoughts

We note that Senge; writing from a combined academic, consultant, and practical position establishes ideal targets and points us in the desirable direction of achieving a successful learning organization that has embraced a systems approach.

Oshry as well points us in the same direction but provides us some observations of not only how to approach the various levels within the organization but also provides us with a crude form of measurement to ensure that we can see the first signs of relationship breakdown. Together we can take the approach that both authors suggest while keeping in mind that the world we live and work in is very messy indeed, and stay on the alert to meet the needs of the individuals making up the organization while monitoring for signs of breakdown that would imperil our success.

One manifestation of our attempt to establish learning organizations is the formation of work teams within our organization. However, the term 'team' has become a 'buzz word' that is often talked about with great authority, yet often misunderstood. Since Senge suggests that teaming is a necessary part of a learning organization, it would do well for us to look at it more closely to ensure that we are sharing a common language.

Teams

We have heard much in recent years on the advantages of teams in the workplace. Many companies have instituted the practice, expended considerable effort and resources on the implementation and most have become very disillusioned with the results. Where teams have worked, the results have been spectacular. The term 'teams' has taken on the attributes of a 'buzz word' without much thought to the commitment that must be made, and the culture that must be present, for them to function effectively.

What are teams?

Most companies assign individuals from several functional areas to a 'team' in order to address a specific cross-disciplinary issue or problem within the organization. During the assignment process, an executive, manager, or supervisor is typically assigned to head the team and members are drawn from various functional disciplines, related to the issue, to contribute to the solution process. This is a good start, but only for an inter-disciplinary work group. A team it is not. Let us examine why these work groups are not a team

- The members are drawn from functional areas and know they will be returning
- Loyalty remains to their parent sub-organizations
- Managers of the parent organization retain administrative control of the individual 'team' members
- Members represent the agendas of their parent sub-organizations
- Activity is frequently directed by the assigned leader

However, if the attributes of a team are present, the work group may transcend these initial limitations and rise through the team building process into a high performance team.

```
┌──────────┐    ┌──────────────┐    ┌──────┐    ┌──────────────┐
│  Work    │───▶│    High      │───▶│ Team │───▶│    High      │
│  Group   │    │ Performance  │    │      │    │ Performance  │
│          │    │ Work Group   │    │      │    │    Team      │
└──────────┘    └──────────────┘    └──────┘    └──────────────┘
```

Adapted from Katzenbach, J. R. (1993) The Wisdon of Teams: Creating the High Performance Organization, Harper Business

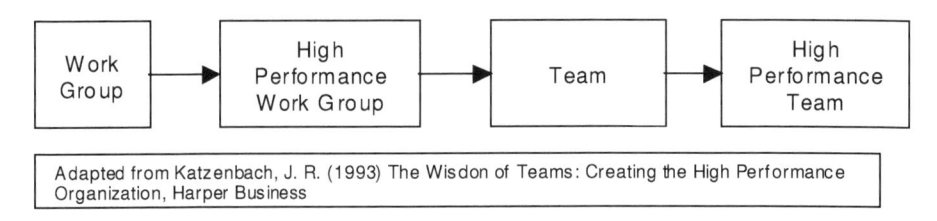

Figure 10. A Progression of Work Groups to High Performance Teams

The key ingredient is trust; bolstered by the attributes of Senge's five disciplines, training in team function techniques, open communications, organizational support, and commitment to the organization. Why then do most organizations that implement team building fail? The need is clear and Katzenbach (Katzenbach & Smith, 1994) in his *Wisdom of Teams: Creating the High Performance Organization*, suggests that teams will be the primary building blocks to creating superior competitive performance in the future. This has been supported most recently by several management researchers with observations that organizations that can learn the quickest, and retain the knowledge with an increasingly fluid workforce, will rise to the top in the fast paced, highly competitive, global operating environment of the future. Senior managers see the need, but frequently do not have a full appreciation of the underlying issues that make a team successful, or are unwilling to devote the time and resources necessary for success.

The process of team building is not a quick or an easy one and teams, given full management support and extensive training will classically progress through the ***Forming - Storming - Norming - Performing - Excelling*** pattern identified by many scholars and practitioners. However, recent studies have cast considerable doubt that each of these phases is distinct and tend to favor a more dynamic approach that the phases are indeed present but there is considerable overlap, so a revised model may actually show the traditional overlaid on the three main steps of team building; *chartering – building - sustaining* seen in a project management environment.

Carl Adams, 2000 – Adapted from Mantel & Meredith

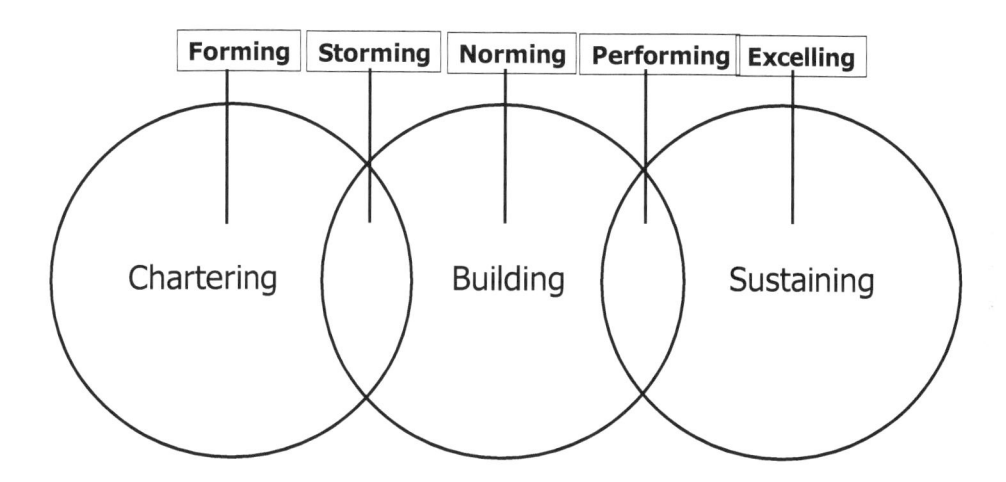

Figure 11. Team Building Process (Used with permission of Carl Adams)

Most teams begin as work groups

Regardless of the title given the group, most teams begin life as a work group in the classical sense. Management appoints a leader and provides functional area experts on a temporary basis to assist in resolving an inter-disciplinary issue that is defined in advance. As the group continues their work, they may find pleasure in the process and, under effective group leadership, find an outlet for their personal store of knowledge. Then, as the group investigates the suspected causes they will test management commitment by gauging the quantity, quality, and depth of the information to which they have access.

In the course of investigating the causal effects of the assigned problem, the group may be given some training in analytical techniques such as Ishikawa Cause and Effect Diagramming, star bursting, and other decision-making approaches. When applying these newly acquired techniques, the group members will inevitably discover areas of less desirable performance. If they ignore these as not being part of their assignment, the group will remain a task group but, if they surface these collateral issues to the group leader and on to the sponsor for action, they will have transitioned to a high performance work group.

High performance work groups

Once having established the group identity as committed to the organization, usually by uncovering issues that they were not tasked to investigate, management may decide to keep the group intact, and assign additional emergent issues. In an organization willing to commit the time and resources members will be rewarded with additional training, and perhaps even outside education, to equip the group with additional tools to function more effectively. The tasks however are still assigned by management via the appointed group leader, and the members still owe their primary allegiance to their functional areas. As more tasks are assigned to the group, the leader may realize that individual members of the group may be better equipped by prior training and experience to lead the task investigation. When the assigned leader voluntarily steps aside, formally or informally, and offers leadership of the investigation to the one most qualified to lead it, the high performance work group transitions to a team.

The beginning of a team structure

Team leaders are usually situational and members of the team, knowing the capabilities of the others, will typically accept leadership from whatever source appears to be the best suited to the purpose. Members begin to contribute voluntarily and will begin to seek out innovative solutions rather than suggesting incremental changes. This signals the transition to situational leadership and a dramatic increase in commitment to the organization.

Management assignment may still continue through an assigned leader, but the internal team organization acknowledges that the assigned team leader is a single point of contact for the convenience of management. The function of the team undergoes a subtle change and issues found in the course of investigations are taken up for solution without referring them outside the team. Generally, the designated point of contact for the team will include additional reports with the required deliverables, and the main characteristic is that individual team members are always credited with the discovery, the work, and the suggestions for implementation.

Defining a high performance team

Transition to a high performance team occurs when individual team members bring issues to the attention of the team that are not discovered in the course of investigation of assigned tasks. Individual members may even bring issues outside the organization for the team to address. High performance teams may even address issues well outside their personal expertise and seek additional information well outside the scope of their assignments in order to better understand the issues involved. For example, it would be characteristic of a plant operations team to seek information on product distribution and consumer appeal to determine if they should address a change in the process to make packaging and shipping processes more effective. At this level, company management may embrace the efforts as valuable to the overall mission, or may begin to see the process as threatening to their personal or collective power base.

Organizational Support

Achieving high performance teams within organizations is not possible without a number of factors:

- Clear vision communicated across all levels of the organization
- Clear, performance based goals
- Open communications throughout the company
- Trust
- Committed employees
- Support for acquisition of knowledge

When all members of the organization are encouraged to grow intellectually, receive support from the company to increase their personal effectiveness, and are committed to achieving the established goals in the most effective and efficient manner, can an environment fostering the formation of high performance teams be achieved. This approach requires long-term commitment, along with dedicated resources, from the highest levels of management to achieve a cultural change in which the attributes of trust, open communication, and commitment can take place.

The Implications of Teams

Forming teams within a project organization is acknowledged to be crucial, especially the group consisting of the project manager and the principal project office team members. Depending on the size and duration of the project, formation of teams may be a viable undertaking and promoted by the project manager beyond the permanent project staff, to include functional managers and perhaps others. The rationale is that time and resources expended to achieve even a high performance work group frequently produces satisfactory results in the form of better cost and schedule outcomes. This rationale extends to any organization that desires to form groups of committed individuals dedicated to the success of the organization while expanding their individual capabilities

As in a project management environment, teams function best in an autonomous state and tend to return the investment many-fold, but over time. If we are aware that the investment includes training of those Oshry calls 'lowers' in the organization and provide them with increasing autonomy, the investment will be successful. However, a real threat may be perceived if we do not enter into the process with full knowledge of the potential for an emerging team to decide to investigate if our compensation package is appropriate to our performance. Threatening indeed!

An organization that is willing to invest in its people and provide an open environment in which they can function as a team will be rewarded, but the process is not comfortable for anyone, yet must be undertaken in order to achieve the goal of a learning organization. You will note that members of a high performance team emerge as situational leaders as the need arises and this fits well with Margaret Wheatley's perception of a 'leader full' organization (Wheatley, 1999).

From Leadership to Followership, At Last

It seems like it took quite a while to get to *followership*, but we did need to establish a foundation upon which to base these thoughts. We are beginning to see that there is much written about what it takes to become a good leader but very little about what it takes to be a good follower. Perhaps this was identified best by Goffee (Goffee, 2001) who refers to earlier work suggesting the progression as *leadership – teamship – followership*. Intellectually it makes sense that a good follower is one who can step forward to become a leader and therefore understands when to take a subordinate role. In the introduction I referred to an awakening to this issue led by a simple question in a workshop.

If we accept the position taken by Goffee as academically sound, let us look closer at application in the real world of profit and non-profit organizations. We have seen that when we establish an organization that fosters an atmosphere of trust, encourages our colleagues and associates to master themselves, and move toward developing a mental model, they are better able to share their vision with others and begin to take a holistic view of the organization and their place in it. We also see that in order to progress from task oriented work groups to teams, the individual members must rise to leadership as the situation dictates and their expertise is needed. We also noted that the organization must provide the support, in the form of training, education, and tools as necessary for the emerging teams to function effectively. As we attain our personal ability to function effectively within high performance teams, or gain *teamship* at an individual level, we develop the ability to make an individual determination of when to rise to a leadership role and when it is best to subordinate ourselves and take on the role of a follower.

How does one know when to allow another individual to take a leadership role? In the usual organization where we are competing for visibility for promotion such an event would be difficult to imagine. However, when we look carefully at a learning organization where individuals have learned to master themselves and can share their personal visions freely in an atmosphere of trust, knowing when to subordinate oneself becomes a relatively easy matter. After all, Harry Truman (1884-1972), former President of the United States stated "It is amazing what you can accomplish if you do not care who gets the credit." And this remains appropriate across all organizational structures, provided foregoing the credit does not adversely impact the individual career.

In leadership workshops, we frequently see emergence of thought that agrees with the principles and theories of the learning organization, systems thinking, and simple solutions to emerging problems but the concept does not seem to be implementable within the organization the workshop members belong to. The interesting point is that when we delve deeper into the issues of why the organization would not support these concepts, it always seems to devolve on someone higher up not being a leader in the sense that we are investigating. We next look at the term followership as being a continuation of leadership and we see wiggling and discomfort in the room and dialogue begins to emerge regarding how to lead, or follow, when the one in charge does not do so. We carefully avoid the term followership.

The choice of words is interesting. There seems to be a negative connotation to the word follower, yet we use it here in a form that would indicate an individual who has not only attained the knowledge and skills necessary be become a leader, but one who is so comfortable with themselves and their ability to take a systems view, that they find no difficulty in voluntarily subordinating themselves to follow the lead of an individual who is best able to fill the position at the time.

Perhaps the term argument should be left alone, but it does strike a chord and seems to open the area for dialogue. In any case the knowledge of the transition is a valuable metric that can assist both the individual and the organization in gauging the progress toward greater organizational effectiveness, and if a mentor is included in the process, these indications could very well indicate success of the process.

Mentorship

When we, as leaders, have matured to a position of followership, we become noticed. In a learning organization it would be natural for a subordinate to seek out the individual for guidance and assistance. This request usually begins the role of mentor, however, in some organizations a more formal approach may exist. However, assuming the relationship of a mentor is an individual decision and one that is not easily revoked.

Relationship is the key.

A mentor assumes a responsibility for ensuring the protégée progresses at a pace that is accelerated, and slightly uncomfortable so as to ensure the maximum benefit from the professional as well as personal experience. The mentor is usually senior to the protégée in the organization but, depending on the quality of the relationship, the process may transcend several promotions and even movement to another organization. Scary; and can appear to be threatening to the organization, unless the concept is clearly understood and accepted.

Time and knowledge transfer are only part of the commitment. Each individual is different and the successful mentor will engage in research and analysis to ensure that the protégée gets the maximum benefit from the experience. Incidentally, the mentor also benefits from this relationship by obtaining a different perspective on the issues and concepts being shared.

Formal, and expected, duties would include:

- Act as advisor on professional and career matters

- Provide access within the organization
- Personalized training, and education
- Encouragement

Advisory Role

The most obvious duty would be to act as an advisor on professional matters both within and external to the organization. This could extend quickly to include membership in professional societies and on occasion, also to fraternal and social organizations as well. The issue here is that what may begin as strictly a professional relationship may result in a less formal one to the mutual benefit of both individuals. In organizations that have adopted a formal or informal lattice structure, this is perhaps less likely as the mentor will have more than one protégée, but the concept is still viable and may materialize. The outcome, in any case, is that the relationship matures to one of mutual trust and respect that enhances the organizational relationship, so should be encouraged.

Providing Access

Providing access within the organization is generally the initial objective of the protégée and cannot be denied. The organization would wish the mentor to ensure that the protégée has the requisite knowledge and skill to be effective in the current assignment and is being groomed for promotion, or for assuming specific responsibilities in a lateral move within the organization. However, if we return to the model introduced by Noel Tichey (Tichey, 1997), we see that the investment in time and effort also results in building leadership skills which create a long term benefit for the organization as a whole. In the interim, the increased internal networking should result in accumulation of better awareness of the organization as a whole and come closer to achieving a systems approach in the decision process.

Training and Education

As the relationship matures and the level of trust continues to grow, the mentor will be in an excellent position to evaluate progress and to suggest additional areas of training, or accumulation of additional knowledge through education, to enhance the personal capabilities of the protégée. Training may be needed, but as it is generally specific and relatively short range, this would usually be recommended by the functional manager and may only be suggested by the mentor. However, the main thrust is the building of leadership and management skills which require more of an educational approach and may take the form of individual research assignments, placement on a cross-disciplinary work group, or even a suggestion to take a few courses at a local university. Frequently this area of responsibility would result in generation of an article in a professional journal or presentation at a conference, which not only enhances the individual resume, but also increases the networking capabilities of the protégée. This remains a risk well worth taking as the benefits to the organization generally outweigh the potential of premature departure.

At an appropriate time in this process, it may be prudent to guide the protégée into a mentorship role as well in order to round out understanding of the concept. We have long known that when one attempts to teach another, the teacher learns at least as much as the pupil. The process should also broaden the scope of knowledge and enhance the organization by moving closer to a learning organization in retaining knowledge internally.

Encouragement

Probably the most overlooked task of the mentor is to provide encouragement to the protégée throughout the process. This becomes increasingly more difficult as the protégée becomes more knowledgeable and comfortable in the role and begins to approach the level of expertise of the mentor in some areas. If the relationship has been strong and a solid level of trust has been established, the benefit to the mentor is the ability to leverage the superior knowledge of the protégée to enhance their own understanding of the process, and often role reversal begins to take place as the relationship turns more to that of collaboration. This is healthy and would indicate very clearly the success of the process.

Encouragement can be supplied from top-down, bottom-up, among peers in the same organization or laterally across multiple organizations. We see this occurring in normal family life and it is really not necessary for us to know very much detail about the reality of the work detail we are encouraging. In a mentor-protégée relationship this encouragement is usually mutual and should be fostered and promoted by the organization as the ultimate beneficiary in a learning organization, is the organization itself. To accomplish this feat, members of the organization must lay aside their egos and recognize that during their tenure, they are but stewards of the assets entrusted to their care.

Stewardship and Servant Leadership

We have been raised to compete, and our entire human structure is based on competition. We compete for the best grades, being the most popular, and as we mature compete for the best position, job, or highest accolades. Competition makes us strong and we can see through our study of economics that it tends to keep prices down and quality up. How can we reconcile our need to be seen as successful while allowing our subordinates to take the credit for their work, while we, their superiors in the organization remain silent and encourage the effort? Yet this is exactly what we must do to ensure the competitive edge of the organization as a whole. We must recognize that while we may head an organization, a portion of it, or are responsible for a process, we are merely stewards of the assets we are charged with, and our people are human capital to also be conserved and encouraged.

Pie in the sky you might say, and perhaps you are right when describing an organization with which you have had experience in the past, but we see that this type of behavior; encouraging our subordinates to participate to their maximum potential and ensuring that they get due credit and reward for their successes is what allows us to be much more successful than if we rely on the traditional method of doing business. Today it is not management, but leadership that counts and part of leadership is allowing the best use of our talent pool to solve emerging problems in a swift and economical manner. Let us examine some of the background of these approaches and see where they will lead us.

Servant Leadership is not new.

Robert Greenleaf writing in 1977 (Greenleaf, 1977) established the leader of an organization as serving the needs of the organization by managing its assets to achieve the desired results. The choice of title as 'servant' allowed a negative connotation to creep in and, as a result, there has not been much desire for ego driven high performers to be seen as servants, or indeed as followers. However, when we look at the attributes of a servant leader, we see an individual who places the well being of the organization above personal aspirations. One could say in the aftermath of the several scandals of the 2001-2003 time period that part of the reason may well be ego and a lack of concern for the human capital that produced the revenue which allowed the ego to flourish.

An example of servant leadership, albeit under different conditions than one sees in the business world, is the training of an officer in the armed forces which stresses the need to take care of the welfare of the troops under that officer's command. This is so ingrained that, when rations are short, officers will refrain from partaking until the troops have eaten. An old story circulating among the military is that of a British Officer ensuring that meager rations were distributed equally among his men, while he sat down to a table set with crisp table linen and crystal to drink a glass of water and eat one-half a biscuit, which was all that remained. When being asked by a correspondent why he did not at least share equally with his men, he replied that his men would need all their energy for the upcoming battle, and he expected to dine much better after the battle was theirs. That officer was a servant leader and although some humor can be derived from the anecdote, that officer was a leader with style. It is common practice in the United States military, as well as the armed services of many other countries, to serve officers after the troops.

Anecdotal the previous story may be, but it is very clear that supervisors, managers, and executives are overhead and usually do not contribute directly to the production of revenue. It is therefore incumbent on them to ensure that those who do produce the product from which revenue is derived are given every consideration and asset required to perform their tasks to the best of their ability. When we use our knowledge of processes to enhance the ability of our workers to produce a better quality product at the least possible cost we are serving our organization and, if we can encourage others to follow these principles, we are servant leaders.

In short, the responsibility of leaders in an organization, wherever placed, is to exercise their best judgment to further the aims of the organization.

Stewardship

A more acceptable term is stewardship, coined by Peter Block (Block, 1995) who made the concepts introduced by Greenleaf more palatable and who took the approach of conservation of assets, including human capital as a desirable trait in organizational leaders. Not so much different than servant leadership but with the emphasis being placed on assets, and the elimination of the negative connotation, the approach began to see introduction into business schools and consequently into the workforce at the managerial level.

Wherever one is placed in the organization, we can exercise our latitude within our prescribed parameters to conserve assets entrusted to our care and apply them appropriately to ensure the greatest production for the lowest cost. One would believe that we are speaking of things alone, but that is not so. If we consider human capital, we must also ensure that we conserve and use these assets in an appropriate manner while allowing this human capital to increase its value through experience, education, and flexibility.

One argument that frequently crops up in dialogue on providing advanced training or education is the cost not being recovered because they will go somewhere else after the training is completed. That does happen, but one must then look at the organization in a holistic way to ensure that we conserve our people assets by providing enough incentive for them to have a propensity to remain rather than leave when given the opportunity. A steward, or servant leader, will see no threat in providing subordinates with better tools with which to perform their work, regardless of the level involved. We remember that the sole aim is to ensure the most effective utilization in order to achieve organizational aims. The leader is merely the instrument to allow the changes that drive excellence to take place, while ensuring that their protégées are imbued with the spirit of the process to assure stewards or servant leaders in the future.

Protégée

Earlier we examined the role of a mentor in an organizational setting and the role of a protégée is so intertwined that we necessarily touched on the relationship as well, so there is a foundation at this point. Previously we looked at the protégée as someone to whom we impart knowledge and provide opportunities, but the role is two-way in that the protégée also has responsibilities in the relationship.

Trust

As the protégée expects trust from the mentor and the organization to tolerate mistakes made in the learning process, the mentor and organization have a right to expect that the protégée will exercise due diligence in the performance of the duties and not allow the latitude for mistakes to act as an excuse for sub-standard performance. In addition, the trust must extend further, for the protégée becomes an extension of the mentor on many occasions and it is incumbent on the individual to honor the trust in not communicating privileged information to unauthorized parties. This is very difficult to do for the temptation to exhibit knowledge outside the scope of our peers is very great, yet we must be diligent in safeguarding the competition sensitive and proprietary information that comes our way as a result of close association.

It is not unusual, especially after some time has passed in the relationship, for the mentor to impart current sensitive information to the protégée for purposes of instruction as well as to obtain feedback or another perspective. When this happens, we must realize that we are being entrusted with information not available to all, and that we become stewards of this information until such time as the mentor releases it, or authorizes us to do so. This level of trust cannot be broken without losing the confidence of the mentor and dissolution of the relationship. If you, the reader, doubt the importance of trust, stop and think about it before continuing further. I cannot conceive a quicker way to end a relationship than by a lack of trust.

Loyalty

A protégée must possess loyalty to the relationship that is in consonance with the trust placed in the individual. This loyalty is both personal and organizational and we must be careful to separate the two. Although they may conflict from time to time, the best judgment of the individual must be used to ensure the conflict is resolved amicably and ethically.

Personal Loyalty

As in the course of any close relationship, we become exposed to the good and the bad in individuals, and we become privy to events and information that are best left confidential. Personal loyalty would suggest that should the protégée become aware of such matters they be treated in a confidential and delicate manner so as to not adversely affect the relationship.

Relationships between a superior and a subordinate, mentor and protégée, or wherever a power distance is present places a responsibility on the mentor to use even personal setbacks as a tool of instruction and the protégée must realize that the object lesson is one that should not be used to disadvantage the mentor. In addition, as the relationship matures, it is not unusual for the protégée to be invited to social events for purposes of exposure, and in these settings may become exposed to information or otherwise gain knowledge that is detrimental to the mentor if made public or even communicated to peers. The protégée must be honor bound to safeguard such confidences to the extent possible under law, although one does hear of confidences being kept in spite of the law at great personal risk.

Needless to say, the mentor also bears joint responsibility to ensure that this loyalty is returned by also keeping inviolate personal aspects of the relationship not adversely impacting the organization.

Organizational Loyalty

Loyalty to the organization is perhaps the easier to understand, but the more difficult to observe. We frequently hear the lament that a long career with a single company is no longer possible, or desirable. We also hear frequently that the organization has no loyalty toward us, so why should we have any loyalty to the organization. Well, the response is not what we might like to hear but is rather pragmatic. While you are getting paid by the organization, or agree to volunteer your time and effort in a non-profit organization, your energies and loyalty is to the organization. As a protégée the organization, or at least your mentor, has enough confidence in your success that they wish to be a part of it, and have dedicated some time and effort to ensuring you become more successful.

What do we mean by being loyal to an organization? Not communicating trade secrets, proprietary or competition sensitive information for starters, but it goes further. The organization has a right to expect your best effort in return for the best effort on the part of the organization. You are free to disagree on what constitutes the best effort, but remember that you may not be privy to all the factors that govern the support you are provided. Your mentor may have made an attempt that has been turned down but, since the mentor is also under an obligation of organizational loyalty, may not feel the need to communicate the attempt to you.

Other than internal factors, you may be faced with comments or enquiries from colleagues or peers at professional meetings and conferences. Your responsibility is to ensure a favorable perspective of your organization, within the boundaries of honesty, of course. In times when you cannot say anything good is it best to show your loyalty by not saying anything at all. After all, the individual to whom you are confiding may be your boss at some time and you can rest assured will remember your breach of loyalty.

Selecting a Mentor

In the absence of a formal mentorship program, or sometimes in spite of one, most protégées will seek their own mentor, be the person a role model or one who is perceived to assist in advancing in the organization. In most cases, the mentor is one who would enable the protégée to obtain a desired objective easier and quicker. What many do not understand is that the bonds formed in a successful relationship transcend the original objective.

Selecting a mentor is not a casual undertaking. The relationship is more of a coaching or teaching one and in many aspects may resemble a parent-child connection. These attributes are healthy and indeed can assist in forming a strong bond that will benefit the protégée, but must be entered into with great care and careful attention to detail. In addition, it is well to remember that the prospective mentor will also be seeking to determine if you are worthy of the investment of time and effort, and have the capability to meet their expectations. Enter the relationship with great care. Getting out could be difficult and could easily be career damaging.

Supervise

Supervision of workers is perhaps the most difficult task in an organization. One must realize that the workers who produce the revenue stream are the very foundation of the organization and everyone else is filling an overhead function that does not contribute to profit. Supervisors fall into rough classifications that have not changed over many decades.

- Established and respected authority
- Administrative supervisor
- Training opportunity

In each case we must carefully weigh the reason for having a supervisor to begin with against the benefit to be derived. As in all matters of leadership and followership, it is the relationship of the individuals involved that create either a favorable or unfavorable atmosphere for achieving the stated objectives of the organization.

Established and Respected Authority

Traditionally, the functional supervisor has risen from the ranks of the workers engaged in the particular task or activity and is an individual that is technically competent, well respected, and capable of carrying out the administrative duties. Of course, this is an ideal, but we see many variations depending on the organizational structure and product involved. Since we will at some point be faced with selecting a supervisor for technically complex work groups, it is essential that we understand the parameters with which we will have to deal, and devise ways to deliver the requirements in the presence of a compromise.

Technical Competence

Workers expect the supervisor to be able to resolve technical issues and to answer detailed questions about processes. They will usually expect the supervisor to have been competent in the performance of similar activities and have a broad experience base on which to draw. Essentially workers would like to see the supervisor as a source of advice on the specific details of accomplishing a task and to quickly identify alternative means of accomplishing a task safely but not necessarily economically.

The perception of the workers will invariably be that the supervisor is their buffer with management and, since the supervisor understands the work and has the position, the supervisor is better able to ensure that management does not assign tasks that are beyond the capability of the workforce to perform. The supervisor must ensure that no action is undertaken that could jeopardize the trust, and that safety issues are fully considered and active steps taken to conserve both material and human assets. Communicating these responsibilities effectively can be challenging yet walking the line between accomplishing the objectives of the tactical planning process while being an effective steward and practicing servant leadership is essential.

Well Respected

The effectiveness of the traditional supervisor is based on the professional respect of the subordinates and is usually enhanced by performance under stress or in emergency situations. The military and the construction industry are excellent examples of earned respect and each field of endeavor has stories of superb performance and professional competence under stressful, often life threatening, conditions. Respect can also be earned by performing a particularly delicate task or operation that presents clear evidence of competence and a command of the technical processes beyond the capability of most of the workers involved. Respect can also be earned by application of study to improve processes, make the tasks easier, or by being recognized as an expert in some area by a professional society in which one operates.

Public recognition of competence is not limited to the ranks of workers and supervisors but extends to managers and professional workers as well. One of the marks of a professional is membership and active participation in a professional society at the local, regional, national, and international levels. Supervisors who are active and hold office in a local body of the professional society, participate actively in the regional and national conferences, by serving on committees, presenting technical papers, or taking on obligations beyond the scope of personal development, also tend to increase their professional reputation and rise in the esteem of those they supervise.

Administrative Capabilities

Supervisors are tasked with administrative duties and must certainly satisfy these requirements in order to perform at a level that is acceptable to the organization. It is interesting to note that this competence must be visible to both the manager and to the workers involved for equitable and appropriate assignment of tasks is perhaps one of the major issues among workers in general. Support can quickly wane for a technically competent and well respected professional who is inept in managing the administrative duties associated with the supervision of a workforce.

Great care must be taken when elevating a superior technical worker to a supervisory position to ensure that the individual is provided with the tools to succeed administratively. The investment in additional training can assist greatly in ensuring increased productivity, especially if included in the training is some assistance in overcoming ego driven emotions and creating an understanding of stewardship and servant leadership. In addition, as this assignment is being contemplated, it would be an excellent time to determine if a mentor relationship would be desirable.

Administrative Supervisor

United States industry has taken the lead in using the supervisory position as a means of making use of superior administrative abilities while relying on a broad technical knowledge base to ensure appropriate assignments, while leaving technical competence issues to be resolved within the workforce under the guidance or final approval of the supervisor. This is not new and many believe it had its beginning with the engineered standards of scientific management at the turn of the 20th Century (Locke, 1982).

The attributes of a successful administrative supervisor would include an analytical ability and some technical education would be appropriate. We see this type of management style most frequently among knowledge workers where the supervisor functions more in the role of a contract administrator to ensure that contractual obligations are met. Additional duties would be to assure that appropriate support personnel are available to ensure the timely delivery of contractually required products.

Research and development activities, consulting companies, and other organizations that depend of knowledge of their workers are appropriate for this type of supervisory approach.

Training Opportunity

Many organizations use supervisory level assignments as a training ground to ensure that entry level management trainees have the people skills to justify continued retention in the organization. This is not as bad as it may sound, for it is not too far a departure from an administrative supervisor, and has the added value of acquainting the manager trainee with the processes that generate the revenue.

When a professionally strong and competent worker is available to assist in the explanation of the processes, and the trainee has a good background in the discipline from a theoretical perspective, this assignment can be rewarding for both the trainee and the workforce being supervised. In some cases, it is an opportunity for the trainee to see how reality compares to theory. In other situations it is an opportunity for the trainee to assist productivity by bringing fresh concepts to an older process. Much depends on the relationship that is established between the supervisor and the workforce.

Relationship to Workers

Ego is the worst enemy of the supervisor!

Professionals, whether blue collar or white, possess skills that are unique and are in demand by the process. Failure to recognize that a supervisory role is best accomplished by achieving harmony and voluntary compliance is generally the precursor to failure. Treating workers with the respect due their skill is an absolute requirement.

One often hears trite phrases that sound politically correct but are absolutely inappropriate in the workplace of the real world. Respect does not imply subservience, nor does seeking advice on technical issues imply abrogation of responsibility. As a supervisor we must harbor a genuine respect for the work performed, yet be quick to note when the work is not to standards so as to take prompt corrective action.

As supervisors we must never forget that we are indeed the buffer between the direct labor that produces the revenue flow and management, but we owe allegiance both up and down the line, and in some cases also laterally as explained earlier by Barry Oshry (Oshry, 1995). Above all we must be very careful to act as a steward to appropriately use the material and human assets of the organization and as a servant leader to adequately represent the workers. How well we discharge these obligations will be noted by both our superiors and our subordinates.

Ego is the worst enemy of the supervisor!

Manage

We return here to the management leadership continuum after having investigated leadership to determine that the real goal should be followership, but with a clear understanding that management functions are absolutely essential to maintaining a viable organization while we exercise our leadership initiatives to make it better. After all, we have to survive today to be around tomorrow. Although managing scarce resources has been around since prehistoric times, we see Frederick Winslow Taylor and scientific management as the beginning of a modern era of management, but it has undergone drastic changes and with several theories vying for our attention we can look at some being of help and others not being able to stand the light of implementation (Lee, 1980).

The 1980's contributed materially to what Peter Drucker referred to as the flavor of the month in management theory and, although each published work reflected an approach that worked well, many managers blindly took the process as a viable prescriptive implementation. They were surprised to find themselves where the other company had been, at best, but did not take them into a competitive position because that spot had already been taken. Those that accepted the approach as a lesson to be learned and were able to apply time honored principles, as well as common sense, progressed much better. However, the world had changed dramatically with the fall of communism and globalization came into full swing (Friedman, 1999) and the competition became fierce, and change in the operating environment much more dynamic.

Probably the emergence of the learning organization (Argyris, 1975) and a systems approach (Senge, 1990; Senge, 1991) heralded the current era of management thought with its concentration on people as the important ingredient in the success of an organization. This approach was enhanced by the addition of project management as a viable and disciplined approach to high risk one-time ventures (Kerzner, 1998) and the acceptance of a philosophy that relied on the embedded expertise of the workforce. Needless to say, there have been many contributions to management thought over the past two decades, and each has brought further light to our approach and allowed us to selectively apply the theories that fit the organization and the circumstances of the particular situation. Several sub-disciplines have evolved as a byproduct of the several managerial approaches, among them the distinction between strategy, or policy, and tactical planning.

Policy

Many models devoted to the process of strategic planning or policy formulation are available and each executive tends to favor the one best understood. Several areas of commonality exist among the several models however, and some omissions which may be of importance to present as well as future leaders in fast-paced, highly competitive, organizations. Areas of commonality invariably separate the process into four distinct general areas:

- Information gathering
- Formulation
- Implementation
- Evaluation and control

And, virtually all are characterized by heavy reliance on processes that are crucial to the success of the strategy or policy:

- Mission or vision
- Feedback loops
- Measures of compliance

Information gathering

Before an attempt is made at developing a strategic plan or long-term policy, a clear understanding of the operating environment, both internal and external, must be present. It is not unusual for managers to have a very clear understanding of their own particular portion of the task or job, especially in a manufacturing process, but an overall view is frequently elusive. Managers depend on their peers in related areas to do their job and to let them know when an adjustment may be necessary in the way their areas interact. Clearly this is not the most effective approach and an effort must be made to obtain a more system like view of the operation internally. This system view of the internal environment is only the first step in the information gathering process for we must also become aware of what our competition and industry as a whole is doing. And, to complicate the process further, we realize that we do not operate in an isolated sphere, but within a larger external environment with divergent

- Laws
- Regulations
- Culture
- Personal preferences

SWOT Analysis

Several methods of analysis have been formulated but perhaps the best known, and most used, is an analysis of Strengths, Weakness, Opportunities, and Threats, or SWOT analysis. This is a very powerful tool for focusing our attention on the specifics of the problem. The model is usually arranged in the form of a grid where strengths and weaknesses are internal representations and opportunities and threats are generated from external sources. The process of obtaining the information is usually referred to as environmental scanning and is as applicable to the internal as well as the external environments.

		External	
		Opportunity	Threat
Internal	Strength		
	Weakness		

Figure 12. Traditional SWOT Analysis Matrix

Of significance in generating information is that there is a distinction of perspective. For example, when we scan the external environment we will generally categorize the findings into opportunities and threats, and then determine whether the company can respond to the opportunity with strength or are too weak to be effective. In long range forecasting, we will attempt to identify the potential environment and then formulate a response that allows us to increase our strength to meet the expected scenario, or develop a course of action to convert our area of weakness to a position of strength. Here we are dealing with OS, OW, TS, and TW. Clearly we always want to meet opportunities from a position of strength and avoid threats when we are weak.

We can also look at the internal strengths and weaknesses of the company and seek an external environment with an acceptable mix of opportunities and threats. Should we determine that our company has strength, perhaps a technological advantage, over our competitors that is unmatched, we can seek out, or even create an external environment that would create an opportunity. In this scenario we are dealing with SO, ST, WO, and WT.

Dynamic SWOT

A newer approach is the use of a dynamic SWOT where we can combine several approaches and, instead of taking a point in time for our SWOT analysis, extend it to include positioning for the future as well. We have found it easier to take a more predictive view and have divided each quadrant in two to allow for a more robust analysis as well as a foundation for more complex analyses.

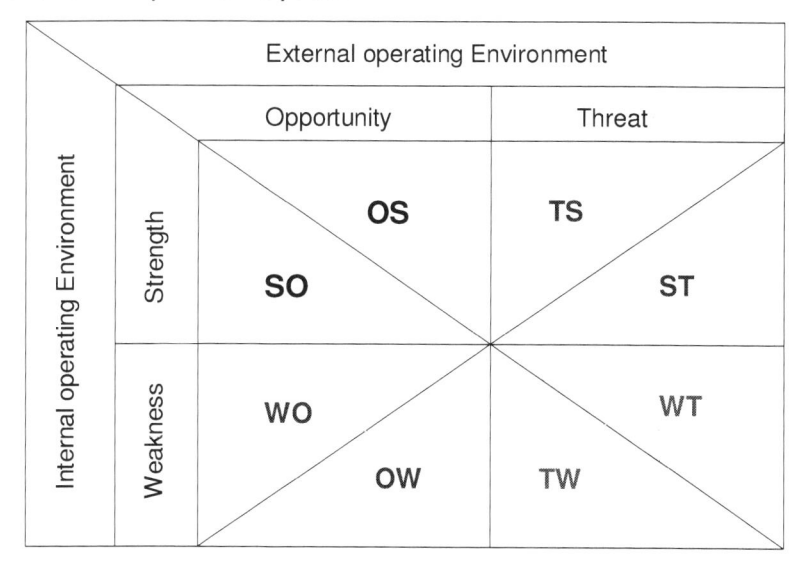

		External operating Environment	
		Opportunity	Threat
Internal operating Environment	Strength	OS / SO	TS / ST
	Weakness	WO / OW	WT / TW

Figure 13. Dynamic SWOT Model

In this SWOT adaptation, we propose that the original static analysis can be more dynamic by adding a predictive ability. For example, in early 1990, it was with an understanding that target customer companies in the external environment were threatened by their weakness in implementing front-end logistics because of what was at that time termed the engineers mentality. This however translated into an opportunity for a fledgling company, if they could only translate their similar engineering focus weakness (OW) into strength (OS) by educating their engineers in management and systems thinking while positioning to take advantage of organizational learning. This approach proved to be highly successful and the company was able to enter a niche market with a unique perspective that reduced customer cost of doing business. As competitors entered the niche market, and threatened the established strength (ST), the company was able to leverage their position by increasing the generalist nature of their service and creating an expanded service offering based on their intimate knowledge and broad based approach to maintaining a strong position and by creating a new opportunity (SO). Some of the competitors followed that lead, added their own innovative ideas, and allowed all to learn together in the Northwest quadrant, while others continued to participate in the southwest quadrant or fell into the southeast quadrant, the one we refer to as "NGT" or 'never go there' and dissolved.

Essentially, we must understand that the pace of business is increasing and managing change is the job. If we consistently continue to use static tools, we will consistently miss the opportunities, fail to see the threats, and quickly fall into the NGT pit. However, this again is one tool that has served well, but you will need to find a better way as this tool is now increasing in popularity and is being applied not only in the United States but in several other countries as well. You will need to look closely at other tools and seek to integrate them with your own internal environment and culture to effectively address emerging challenges in your competitive environment.

Formulation

Policy formulation is usually in response to our findings resulting from environmental scanning. For example, in Strength – Threat scenario a company develops a process to fill a particular military need that is so innovative that it cannot be easily matched by competition. However, the export regulations of the country prohibit sales of the technology outside the country. The company can then invest in efforts to change the regulation to permit exports, or seek an exemption that will serve the same purpose. This scenario recognizes an opportunity to match the strength of the company and a policy to convert the threat to expansion of the business is formulated. Seldom does a company have a single issue to pursue and a number of objectives, and strategies to achieve the objectives must be developed into policies that do not conflict. A clear vision or mission statement assists in ensuring that policy conflicts are minimized.

Implementation

Once a clear objective, or concept, is determined, the decision of how to best implement the strategy must be addressed. Typically, a project management approach is utilized because it is an accepted method of implementing complex strategy. During the planning stage, a proposal is developed which addresses projected beginning and completion times, estimated costs, and identifies required resources. Of significance, and often overlooked, is the need to establish metrics to evaluate progress concurrently with the development of the plan. Suggested modifications to the objective may also be made during this phase, and often required due to changes in the internal or external environments. On approval, and coordination of required resources with other pending projects, the proposal is accepted and the work to achieve the objective begins in earnest.

Evaluation and control

Environmental scanning continues throughout the project because it makes little sense to continue to expend resources to meet an objective that is no longer contributing to the vision or mission of the company. The goal here is to conserve resources by terminating a project at the earliest possible time when the objective no longer conforms to the overall company strategy. In addition, constant monitoring of project progress is essential to ensure that the allocated resources are being utilized appropriately and that advancements in technology are being incorporated, where feasible, to improve schedule and reduce cost in achieving the objectives. Of importance here is to modify the measurement criteria to incorporate advancements in technology and state-of-the-art processes. Of course, as the objective is achieved, there must be a logical and effective closing process to return resources to other projects and to terminate the existing processes.

Clearly this process must be communicated clearly at all levels of the organization and input to an overall strategy solicited. Frequently we find that solutions to very complex problems faced by upper level managers appear as having very simple solutions to employees actually engaged in the task of implementing the strategy. The real problem seems to be that upper managers do not usually take the time to ask the question. Perhaps we need to understand that frequently it is not the search for the solution that is important, but in framing the appropriate question to investigate. The process of setting objectives and developing strategies to meet these objectives is a complex process that can be best addressed from a position of systems thinking and tapping the full potential of the learning organization. (Kerzner, 2001)

Management in Action

There are many ways to effectively manage and we must remember that we manage at many levels in an organization, just as we lead and follow at all levels. Regardless of where we find ourselves, we have an opportunity to acquire new skills, refine older ones, and contribute to the success of our organization and consequently ourselves.

Learning Throughout The Process

As we moved through the concepts presented in this volume, we hope that you have found

- An appreciation for the complexity of our operational environment
- An understanding that there are many tools and concepts available for our use
- Developed a thirst for knowledge
- Embarked on a personal development program
- Recognized that there is no single right way to do anything

Several disciplines make up the science or more appropriately the art, of management. Today these management sciences are insufficient to cope with the rapidly changing global environment. As Thomas Friedman stated in his 1999 book, *The Lexus and the Olive Tree*, "The world is 10 years old. It was born when the wall fell in 1989 ..." (Friedman, 1999) Because of this true globalization and the ever increasing access to communications, it is no longer possible for companies to enjoy protected niches and competition comes from the most unexpected places. Scanning the external environment is no longer an annual task; it is one that must be continuous. Scanning the environment was once the task of upper management; today it is the responsibility of every worker. Of interest is that the worker in today's environment is frequently as well aware of the external environmental implications on the company as are the managers, and executives. As our workers become more knowledgeable in research methods, in some cases we find them more aware of issues well before upper management becomes attentive of potential threats or opportunities. Harnessing this low-cost research potential may well become the next challenge for learning organizations.

We know that sustaining an implementation of the five disciplines is not an easy task as Peter Senge states in his 1999 *Dance of Change* (Senge et al., 1999) yet realize that without making the effort to communicate the need for every member to acquire the tools of the five disciplines, we cannot compete successfully in the long-term. We know that as managers, we are busier than ever and long days and short weekends are a fact of corporate life. We also know that we must devote the time to building leaders within our organizations as suggested by Tichey (Tichey, 1997), and we must promote free and open communication at all levels of the organization.

Applying the tools of strategic management, policy formulation, and involving all stakeholders, is an absolute necessity for the continued survivability of the firm, and can no longer be relegated to experts in an obscure group of planners working for the chief executive officer. The methods must be made available to all in the organization and the assistance of each employee harnessed to assist in scanning the internal and external environments.

Technology drivers can frequently speed the processes that are causing critical path problems, and we must take the time to find, evaluate, and implement them without adversely affecting meeting the objectives. Again, here we must foster an openness that will encourage employees to assist by their commitment to the organization. Further, we must foster this commitment in spite of the propensity of employees for higher rates of voluntary employee turnover and less loyalty to the firm.

The challenges are many, but so are the tools. Unfortunately all the low hanging fruit has been picked and we must apply measures that are more time consuming, more difficult, and more innovative to achieve both functionality and quality. We must encourage by example, our quest for further knowledge in all areas related to our profession, as well as professions on the periphery, that contribute to our performance. We must constantly evaluate our successes as well as our failures to determine why we failed, or what we could have done to succeed more effectively. Most importantly, we must approach each task, no matter how trivial, with the mental set that it is up to us to be as effective and efficient as possible in the execution of that task. And, we must encourage all around us to do so.

We sincerely hope that we have sparked your interest and that you have more questions than answers as you reach the end of this volume. Only when we recognize our ignorance in an area do we make our mind available for new ideas and allow ourselves to roam freely to select more dynamic and appropriate approaches to solving emerging issues.

References

Argyris, C. (1975). Leadership, Learning, and Changing the Status Quo. *American Psychological Association,* 33-47.

Bertalanffy, L. (1969). *General Systems Theory.* New York: George Braziller.

Block, P. (1995). Stewardship. 1 ed.,). San Francisco, California: Berrett-Koehler Publishers, Inc.

Capra, F. (1996). *The Web of Life: A New Scientific Understanding of Living Systems.* New York: Anchor Books.

Checkland, P. (1993). *Systems Thinking. Systems Practice.* New York: John Wiley & Sons, Ltd.

Checkland, P. (1999). *30-Year Retrospective.* New York: John Wiley & Sons, Ltd.

Cheng, N. (1997). Shanghai: Your Entry to China. *Washington CEO, 8*(11), 66-72.

Friedman, T. L. (1999). *The Lexus and the Olive Tree.* New York: Farrar Straus Giroux.

Goffee, R. J. G. (2001). Followership. Harvard Business Review Vol. 79(11), 148. Harvard Business School Publication Corp.

Greenleaf, R. K. (1977). *Servant Leadership: A Journey Into the Nature of Legitimate Power and Greatness.* New York, NY: Paulist Press.

Katzenbach, J. R., & Smith, D. K. (1994). The Wisdom of Teams: Creating the High-Performance Organization. New York, NY: HarperCollins.

Kerzner, H. (1998). *Project Management: A Systems Approach to Planning, Scheduling, and Controlling.* New York: John Wiley & Sons.

Kerzner, H. (2001). *Project Management.* New York: John Wiley & Sons.

Lee, J. A. (1980). *The Gold and the Garbage in Management Theories and Prescriptions.* Athens, Ohio: Ohio University Press.

Locke, E. A. (1982). The Ideas of Frederick W. Taylor: An Evaluation. *Academy of Management Review, 7*(1), 14-24.

Nolan, J. S. (1984). Followership Greater Than or Equal to Leadership. *Education, 104*(3), 311-312.

Oshry, B. (1995). *Seeing Systems: Unlocking the Mysteries of Organizational Life.* San Francisco: Berrett Koehler.

Senge, P. M. (1990). *The Fifth Discipline: The Art and Practice of the Learning Organization.* San Francisco: Berrett Koehler.

Senge, P. M. (1991). Learning Organizations. *Executive Excellence, 8*(9), 7.

Senge, P. M. (1994). *The Fifth Discipline Fieldbook.* New York: Doubleday.

Senge, P. M. (1996). Systems Thinking. *Executive Excellence, 13*(1), 15-16.

Senge, P. M., Kleiner, A., Roberts, C., Ross, R., Roth, G., & Smith, B. (1999). *The Dance of Change: The Challenges to Sustaining Momentum in Learning Organizations.* New York: Currency- Doubleday.

Tichey, N. M. (1997). *The Leadership Engine: How Winning Companies Build Leaders at Every Level.* New York: Harper Business.

Weidenbaum, M. (1998). The Bamboo Network: Asia's Family-Run Conglomerates. *Policy,* (10), 59-65.

Wheatley, M. J. (1999). *Leadership and the New Science: Discovering Order in a Chaotic World.* San Francisco: Berrett-Koehler.

Wheatley, M. J., & Kellner-Rogers, M. (1996). *A Simpler Way.* San Francisco: Berrett-Koehler Publishers.

About the Author

Dr. Seteroff is retired as President of Management & Logistics Assoc., Inc. of Poulsbo, Washington and continues involvement with portions of the business in a part time and consulting capacity. He has earned a Doctor of Business Administration (Management) degree from Nova Southeastern University in 1997. His dissertation was a study of voluntary employee turnover among professional engineers. He is an adjunct professor for the Bangor Academic Center of Chapman University, in economics, organizational leadership, and strategic management and serves as practitioner faculty for the University of Phoenix both online and at the Washington Campus. He is also an adjunct instructor for City University in economics, business, and project management. He served as the General Chairman of the International Logistics Conference in 1998, and as the Coordinating Chairman of the Advanced Technology Steering Group from 1991 to 1998. He also served as a member of the collaborative research committee in the Practitioner Series of the Academy of Management between 1998 and 2000. Research interests remain in voluntary employee turnover among highly skilled professionals, and include the effects of advanced technology implementation on the strategic posture of high performance organizations. He resides in Quilcene, Washington.

ISBN 1412008166